Mandarin Hip Hop

嘻哈说唱学汉语

4

卢毓文 著
Sarah Lu

北京语言大学出版社
BEIJING LANGUAGE AND CULTURE UNIVERSITY PRESS

致 谢

Acknowledgements

My sincerest thanks go to the following friends whose patience, advice and encouragement have made these books possible: Serena Jin, George and Barbara McDonald, Alex Sommerville, Pam Stanley, Jane Shanahan, Julie Cheung, Ingrid Yip, Helen Chiang, Byron Wong, 吕柏熹，蔡孝宁，林荣耀，蒋立恩，林继君，曾宪章，谈蜀华，卢克自，姚俊儒，袁美 and all the staff at Beijing Language and Culture University Press. A special thanks to Prof. Mark Manno who has devoted his time to proofreading the whole series of books and has given me many valuable suggestions. Without him, these books would not be possible.

The CD recordings containing action songs, bilingual chants and mnemonic rhymes are the marvelous joint effort of my colleagues and children from both Taiwan and Glenealy School of Hong Kong.

Dedicated to all my current

and former students for their valuable feedback

and boundless inspiration.

目　录
CONTENTS

录音目录

Contents of the Audio CD

01	Introduction		片头
Spoken Chinese			
02	Lesson 1	Tones	声调
03	Lesson 2	Single finals	单韵母
04	Lesson 3	Compound finals	复韵母
05	Lesson 4	Combined finals I	结合韵（一）
06	Lesson 5	Combined finals II	结合韵（二）
07	Lesson 6	Nasal finals	鼻韵母
Written Chinese			
08	Lesson 7	PARTS	部件
09	Lesson 8	Twenty radicals	二十个部首
Festivals			
10	Lesson 9	Chinese New Year is coming	新年到
11	Lesson 10	Dragon Boat Festival	端午节
12	Lesson 11	Mid-Autumn Festival	中秋节
Animals & Plants			
13	Lesson 12	We like animals	爱护动物
14	Lesson 13	On Mt. Ali	阿里山上
Bags			
15	Lesson 14	My schoolbag has gone	书包不见了
Counting			
16	Lesson 15	Count to 10	数到十
17	Lesson 16	Going shopping	买东西
Emotions			
18	Lesson 17	Don't get angry	别生气
Feelings			
19	Lesson 18	The rickshaw	三轮车
Geography			
20	Lesson 19	Place names of China	中国地名
History			
21	Lesson 20	Chinese dynasties	中国朝代

Music

22 Lesson 6	23 Lesson 8	24 Lesson 9	25 Lesson 10
26 Lesson 11	27 Lesson 12	28 Lesson 14	29 Lesson 18

Don't overlook use of the music to facilitate learning the lesson content. Using the chants and songs makes the learning process both more efficient and lots of fun!

课程概览
Curriculum Overview

Objectives

After completing *Mandarin Hip Hop IV* along with its associated *Workbook*, the student should be able:

- to increase their vocabulary by over 200 words to compose simple sentences correctly for conversational use as illustrated in the individual rhymes and songs;
- to be aware of and appreciate Chinese culture and related celebrations introduced in the individual lessons;
- to recognize around 167 frequently used characters, of which 8 are ranked in the list of the top 100 most frequently used characters, 14 are ranked between 101-200, 89 are ranked between 201-1000, and the remaining 56 frequently used characters are ranked above 1001;
- to follow the correct stroke order in writing at least 167 characters, of which 31 are also used as radicals within other characters.

Materials

The materials chosen are of immediate practical use for the student, and provide a good grounding for further studies. The topics of study of all levels are arranged in alphabetical order to facilitate easy recall, e.g. "A" for Animals & Plants and "B" for Bags, etc. However, units may be taught in any order at the teacher's discretion.

Character Writing	Main Radicals	Sound Indicators	Total
把同动从能民得又无声花最部常 船物树运带别战长比草处相啊便 机笑车各河加代元音衣欧爱呀送 深法旁穿春福武神钱服饭教唱歌 公爷爬叔哥算非区单语油牙苹电 碗首床铁红兴秋节遍端纪念园护 养狗乐阿票冰奶司姐弟妹客椅皮 肚奇怪黄江湖广省朝帝休夏云姨 鹅快杯澳埃及区洲乌龟假娃缸盆 碟浅形艺术武铜钢闹糕嫦娥粽袋 比赛尝赏伴庆祝熊猫犬陆今钞陪 贵找宜客戏椅轮吉秦汉唐宋冬	雨 冰 王 广 示 衣 米 皿 酉 页 彳 犬 贝 羽 母 元 音 无 非 欠 龟 牙 首 止 斤 舟 皮 车 工 云 士	非 单 我 公 夷 夬 由 奥 苗 区 平 果 化 圭 戋 乙 因 同 失 冈 斤 工 吉 宗 代 尝 相 元 勿 反 句 勾 云 票 占 倍 昌 皮 弟 可 艮	8 in top 100 14: 101-200 13: 201-300 27: 301-500 49: 501-1000 56: 1001-
8+14+13+27+49+56=167	31	41	167
The student will recognize approximately 200 words and phrases in the textbook and workbook, including the above radicals and sound indicators.			

序 1 Preface 1

"What is the first thing that a baby does when it comes into the world?" Sarah Lu asks in one of the beginning lessons of her new language manual entitled *Mandarin Hip Hop*. The baby cries. And with that very first cry, the newborn begins to communicate and establishes bonds with the people who are nearby rejoicing at that piercing squeal. And, soon to follow that cry will be the baby's first giggle and laugh, an expansion of its sound repertoire with which it expresses its needs, fears and happiness. With more giggles and cries, a child mimics the adults, experimenting with various strange sounds and associating them with things and deeds in the surrounding world. A mother tongue begins as a foreign language, a speech that a child learns through imitations and repetitions. The learning is never short of challenges, but each challenge is surely to come with fun and appreciation. Fun invites participation and fun promises gratification. No fun, no gain. Fun is indeed the key that characterizes Sarah's philosophy in teaching and learning Chinese, a language whose graphic and tonal complexities are often found to be an ultimate challenge to linguistic sophistication.

As her book title indicates, Sarah teaches through chants and songs in the language manual. Children have a natural inclination for music. With its rhythmic flow from word to word, language readily translates into music. Sarah makes a special effort to evoke that musicality in speech and turns it into a source of motivation and enjoyment in language learning. She chooses popular musical tunes and folksy chant patterns for winsome Chinese lyrics that she composes herself. She correlates the musical pitch with the particular tone of a Chinese word, a skillful design that enables easy acquisition of lexical tones. She mix-matches the Chinese lyrics with English words and phrases, and offers the combinations as mnemonic reminders of vocabulary. She builds complex sentence patterns into seemingly simple chants that help to consolidate the structural foundation in grammar. She tells stories that highlight cultural particulars, including social, historical and geographical information that is crucial to meaningful conversation, especially with native speakers. The CD recordings that accompany the texts are essential performances by bilingual children, an arrangement that cheerfully invites students to join in and sing along. In short, Sarah makes learning Chinese fun rather than a chore.

Music is a universal language that begins with our first cry and laugh. It appeals to all of us, young and old alike, with its spontaneity and powerful expression of feelings. Sarah carries that scribbling wand and unlocks the magic of learning a foreign language through music and words. The importance of musical games to language pedagogy has been more than abundantly noted in the field, but *Mandarin Hip Hop* represents the first, full-scale work in Chinese language pedagogy to bring that approach to fruition. Sarah is blessed with an ear for music and a mind of incredible imagination. We are grateful for what she is sharing with us in this wonderful publication and we look forward to her next project that will take us further along in her enjoyable expeditions.

张洪年 (H. Samuel Cheung)
Professor of Chinese Language and Literature
The Chinese University of Hong Kong
February 2, 2006

序 2　Preface 2

卢毓文老师编写的《嘻哈说唱学汉语》是供儿童学习普通话的汉语教材，包括四册课本、四套配套练习本，并配有精心制作、附有词曲演唱及伴唱乐曲的光盘。每册课本分二十课。

该教材的最大创意在于把儿童汉语学习教材编成了儿童歌谣。请看第一册第一、二两课课文：

第一课　跟我说

听！听！听！
听我说。
说什么？普通话。

说！说！说！
跟我说。
说什么？普通话。

第二课　大家一起听

我说，你不说，
你说，我不说。
大家一起听他说。

我说，你不说，
你说，我不说。
大家一起听一个人说。

该教材也体现了一种新的教学法：先以静态的卡通漫画来引发学生的学习兴趣，再以动态的嘻嘻哈哈、说说唱唱让学生反复练习，与此同时，采用“说唱—拼读—听读识字—集中阅读与识字”的进阶学习法，从而引导学生进行全方位的听、说、读、写训练。

该教材在文字处理上也跟香港一般的汉语教材不同，作者针对目前国际学校（香港）的实际情况，采用了中英文对照、汉字与拼音并容这样的方式。这也有利于教材有较为广泛的适用面。当然，从发展的角度说，是否一定要中英文对照，是否一定要汉字（繁简体）与拼音并容，这可能会随着时间的推移而有所改变。

该教材的作者卢毓文老师长期从事对儿童的汉语教学，她随时注意教学经验的总结，注意教学质量的提升。该教材就反映了卢毓文老师的教学经验，体现了卢毓文老师的教学思想，那就是“寓教于乐”。实践将会证明，卢毓文老师走的路是对的，而且不只对汉语教学，对其他学科的儿童教学也将会有借鉴作用。

是为序。

陆俭明
北京大学教授
世界汉语教学学会会长
2006年4月

序 3 Preface 3

卢毓文女士毕业于高雄师范大学，后负笈美国专攻教育科技。自1974年起，先后在台湾、美国、香港、西澳的大中小学任教，并担任香港国际学校（Hong Kong International School）与香港加拿大国际学校（Canadian International School of Hong Kong）中文部的创办主任，目前为香港英基己连拿小学（Glenealy School, English Schools Foundation）中文学科主任。

卢女士不但擅长对外汉语教学，也曾创办"活力中文教研所"（Living Mandarin），为各大公司设计普通话教程及培训员工，并于20世纪80年代就为香港大学的专业进修学院开办香港唯一的汉外师资培训课程，为期十余年。卢女士多年来除经常参加学术会议并发表论文之外，时有专著，早年的两张儿歌专辑唱片，近年的《国字演进卡》（1-6册）(Chinese Character Evolution Cards Vol. 1-6)、有声套书 *Teach Yourself Living Mandarin Vol. 1-3* （《自学普通话》（1-3册））、《汉语拼音》等，皆获国内外一致好评。

与一般教师相比，卢女士最难能可贵的是她敬业乐业的精神和好学不倦的态度，虽然资深，仍努力不懈，心中琢磨、脑里盘旋的，莫不以如何改进汉语教学为念。本书以语言学、教育心理学及音乐专业为出发点，特别为双语幼儿、小学生及初中生编写设计了全套四册、共80课的韵文并穿插大量会话的歌曲。

这套书不但适于"校本教材"的学校作为补充教材，也适于"主题为本"的学校用作主要教材。本书的特点如下：

1. 每课先以静态的漫画引起学习动机，再以动态的嘻哈说唱贯穿练习，经由"说唱—拼读—听读识字—集中阅读与识字"的进阶学习法，可把学生逐步由"唱说听"导向"认读写"。

2. 根据权威资料选用高频字，以颜色标明级别；词汇适量递增，重现率高。

3. 所附光盘兼有词曲演唱及伴唱乐曲等内容，除课堂使用之外，也适于集会或舞台演出。书中绝大多数儿歌乃专为词语、句法、文法或语文知识教学而创的新作；歌曲主旋律和谐悦耳，音区恰当，音阶流畅，语料词汇丰富。不论词、曲，皆经长年实践改进并延请音乐专家审定制作。

4. 重视记忆术的运用，有些配上汉字图解，宜古宜今；有些参照英文语义，中西合璧，例如用来辅助学习方向词的"你对了"、"上下左右指一指"，曲中"You are right"之right 在英文即属双关语；而教"女"字时，古装妇女与现代芭蕾舞女郎并列，务求达到左右逢源、跨越文化鸿沟的效果。

5. 练习题资料新颖，别出心裁，由浅入深，循序渐进，只要善加利用，按提示发挥，就可以使教学事半功倍。

卢毓文女士曾客居并执教于北半球的美洲及南半球的澳洲，又在两岸三地从事华文教研工作逾三十年，因而在教材编写、课程设计方面，经验丰富，态度认真。在抄袭成风、罔顾版权的今天，看到如此讲求质量、生动活泼的儿歌面世，诚属可喜可贺，特为之序。

金圣华
香港中文大学翻译学荣休讲座教授
香港翻译学会会长
2006年4月

推荐序

卢毓文老师用音乐和童真的想象力把学习中文变成了游戏和娱乐。从脑神经科学看，完全符合左右两脑并用，以及用喜悦情绪强化记忆的原则。书的另一特点是吸收了学生对汉字形象的观感，内容于是并非从上至下的授教，而是网络2.0年代的众志成城模式，更容易贴近用者的需要。非母语学生会因而获益，自不待言。但这种教学方法，对象不应该只是外籍学生。我希望卢老师下一本书会是为本土学生写的。否则，真的会是“肥水流入外人田”，太可惜了！

脑科医生黄震遐
香港脑科基金会主席
2007年12月

Endorsement

By using music and imagination, Ms. Sarah Lu has transformed Chinese language learning into games and entertainment! From a neurological point of view, this is consistent with the idea of using both the left and right brain, as well as reinforcing memory through positive emotion. The other distinctive feature of her book is to incorporate her students' perception of Chinese orthography. Thus this is not top-down didactic approach, but more like a web 2.0 participatory approach which increases user friendliness. It goes without saying, therefore, that second language learners will benefit greatly from her method. However, those who benefit from this strategy should not just be foreign students. I do hope that Ms. Lu will design her next book for students who are native Chinese speakers, so they may also share the richness of her talent!

Huang Chen Ya
Neurologist
Chairman, Hong Kong Brain Foundation
December 2007

作者序

Author's Preface

感谢先祖的智慧，发明了如此神奇瑰丽的语言，使得汉语儿歌音韵天成，特别悦耳；汉语以（象形）字为基本结构单位，如诗如画，是另外一个精妙之处。以双语韵文为主导，结合记忆术与中文手语，令师生双方皆可受惠的 Lunar Approach 一直是我所奉行而又无往不利的教学法。

韵文儿歌向来备受语文教师的推崇喜爱，最新教研报告也强调，音乐旋律对脑部发展、记忆力和注意力的提高都有显著的帮助，可以引起动机、增加趣味性、操练句型、帮助记忆等，史有定评，众所公认；双语对照的韵文就更是好教易学了。“不动手、不入脑”，只有通过写与画才能加强汉字理解力、提升记忆力，才是帮助初学者认写、牢记汉字的有效入门方法。目前由于供外籍儿童学习中文的教材比较缺乏，我愿意把多年的经验提供给同业们作为参考。

本教程遵循“文从语、字随文”的原则循序渐进，汉字方面采用“字本位”教学法，两者并举互动内容，偏重生活题材及日常用语。词汇方面先教高频字词，以利学以致用；单元主题依字母序编列，以便联想查找。书中插图乃精心设计，字中有画，画中有字，往往画中还有话题，便于说话练习。主要适用对象是母语非汉语的中小学生，课时较多的学校（Pre-IB or Pre-AP）可作为兼用教材，课时较少的学校可作为主要教材。

本教程根据语言学、教育心理学、脑神经学、儿童画及音乐专业的教学观，以寓学于乐的双语韵文教学法务实地设计成繁简兼备的教材，分别由北京语言大学出版社与香港资优出版社出版。其精义可由以下几个词首字母所组成的关键字 LUNAR 所涵盖。

Less is more	– 质重于量，贵精不在多
Use it or lose it	– 学以致用，不用则废
No fun no gain	– 寓学于乐，有声有色
Action songs, bilingual chants	– 双语游戏活动
Rhythm	– 韵文说唱

本教程目标包括：

1. 通过八百多个常用词语，奠定良好口语基础。
2. 运用记忆术等实用有趣的方式，帮助学生理解、记忆四百多个常用汉字。
3. 透过好教易学的教材教法，使学生在潜移默化中了解中华文化。
4. 因势利导，循序渐进，培养学生的学习技巧，以利日后进修或自学。

本书具有以下特点：

1. 教学法方面，笔画部首的释形图解新颖到位、浅显易懂，比传统的汉字结构分析更适合外国儿童及青少年学习，可以帮助学生奠定良好的汉字基础。

2. 教材方面，借嘻哈说唱的儿歌顺理成章地导入听读识字，可帮助学习者在没有压力的情况下，通过字词形音义的一再重现，轻松愉快地将所学材料深植入脑，同时提高语文能力。

3. 课程设计上，以善用教学双方的时间精力为念，力图以精简的字数和篇幅，获得最大的学习成效并提升学生的自学能力，因此课时虽有限，启发却无限。

本教材共四级，每级包括课本（附CD一张）及练习册。CD内容分两种形式，有供聆赏的演唱或说唱，也有供练唱、集会或舞台演出的伴奏。前两级各有两本练习册：A 本活动练习本与课本配套使用，有助于复习及操练重点；B 本加强汉字练习本，可按部就班地识字写字，根据一些师生的使用经验，即便是初学汉语的成人也能获益。到第三、四级，则随着儿童心理的发展和学力的进步，A、B本合编为一本综合练习册。

只要紧扣教学重点，从实际出发，灵活应用学生日常生活中最常见的素材，结合视觉与听觉同步协调发展，以嘻哈说唱提高学习动机，借写写画画增进学习效率，尽情发挥图解汉字的功能，帮助学生逐步贯通听、说、认、读、写、打印的具体教学过程，必能达成“说唱写画意难忘，学以致用更灵光”的状态。

自拙作付梓以来，得到不少令人鼓舞的赞许和美言，衷心感谢！不足之处尚祈垂教与指正。希望使用本书的师生都能享有在快乐中学习、在惊喜中发现进步的亲身体验，愿共勉之。

卢毓文 Sarah Lu

2008年12月

Lesson 1 声调

1.1 Rhyme

有 a 不放过，
无 a 找 o e。
iu 和 ui 标在后，
单个元音不用说。

八 bā
口 kǒu 跟 gēn
六 liù 岁 suì

小 i，小 i，不用一点，
j q x 和 ü 没有两点，
l n 和 ü 要写两点。

弟 dì 听 tīng 子 zǐ
句 jù 去 qù 学 xué
绿 lǜ 女 nǚ

- If the vowel "a" appears, it receives the accent. Next look for "o" or "e".
- If there are two vowels, either "iu" or "ui", the tone mark always falls on the second vowel.
- If the tone mark falls on the letter "i", then the dot above "i" is omitted.
- If the sound "j", "q" or "x" is followed by " ü " (e.g. jù, qù), the two dots above " ü " are omitted because in Mandarin, "j", "q" or "x" is never combined with the sound of "u".
- A word in *pinyin* beginning with "l" or "n" and followed by the sound of "ü" must have the two dots above " ü " to distinguish the sound of " ü " from the sound of "u" (e.g. lǘ [donkey] vs. lú [stove]).

Shēngdiào

Yǒu a bú fàngguò,
Wú a zhǎo o e.
iu hé ui biāo zài hòu,
Dāngè yuányīn búyòng shuō.

Xiǎo i, xiǎo i, búyòng yì diǎn,
j q x hé ü méiyǒu liǎng diǎn,
l n hé ü yào xiě liǎng diǎn.

Tones

Don't let go of a,
Look for o and e if there's no a,
Either iu or ui, the tone mark
always falls on the second vowel.
Single vowels, "a piece of cake!"

Lower case i doesn't need a dot,
j, q or x preceding ü doesn't
have 2 dots,
l or n with ü must have 2 dots.

1.3 Fun time

TONE

The acronym "TONE" helps the learner to remember important facts about modern spoken Chinese.

Tonal language How many tones are there in Mandarin?	声调语言
Official language What is the official language of China?	官方语言
Non-alphabetical language Are there more languages that use alphabets than those that do not?	非字母语言
Easy *pinyin* and 4 tones only Is Chinese very difficult to learn?	简易拼音与四声

ˉ	ˊ	ˇ	ˋ
	Yes?	Well...	Fine!
(level)	(rising)	(falling and rising)	(falling)
tā 他	lái 来	wǒ 我	qù 去
wū 屋 (house)	wú 无 (without)	wǔ 五 (five)	wù 物 (item)

轻声　The neutral tone

The neutral tone appears only after another word (or words) using the regular Mandarin tones. It is soft, weak and short. No tone mark is used.

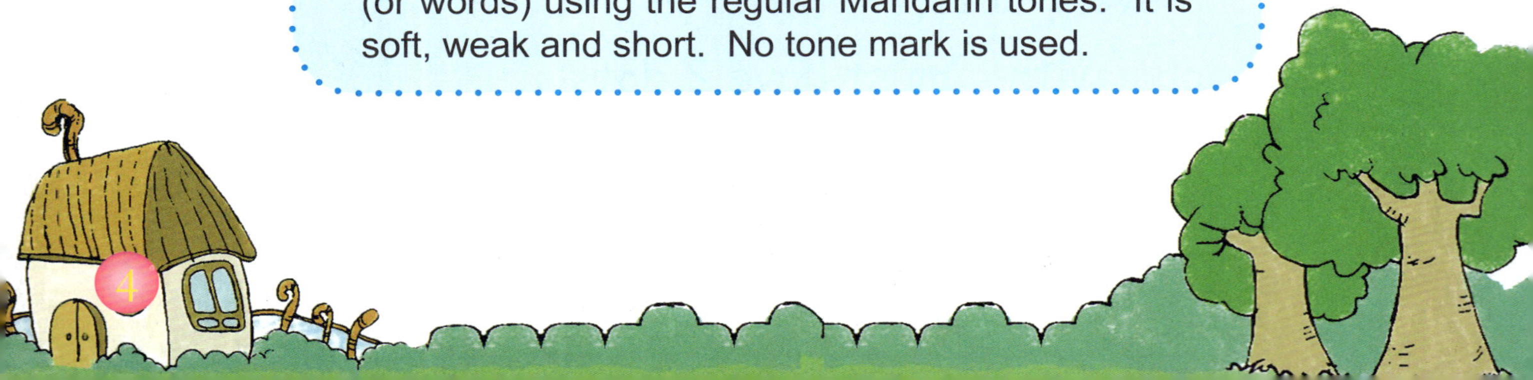

1.4 New words

1. 声调	shēngdiào	tone
2. 放过	fàngguò	let go
3. 无	wú	not have, without
4. 找	zhǎo	look for, search
5. 标	biāo	mark, sign
6. 单个	dāngè	single
7. 元音	yuányīn	vowel
8. 点	diǎn	dot
9. 语言	yǔyán	language
10. 官方	guānfāng	official
11. 非	fēi	not
12. 字母	zìmǔ	alphabetical letters
13. 简易	jiǎnyì	simple and easy
14. 与	yǔ	and, with

1. What does Mandarin literally mean? What was its origin?
2. Among Mandarin, Cantonese, and Shanghainese, which one is the official language in China?
3. What is the difference between the official language and other dialects?
4. Can Chinese people who speak different dialects understand each other?
5. Do all the different dialects have their own writing systems?

Answers:

1. The word Mandarin comes from 满大人, which literally means "Manchu high official". It is now referred to as 普通话, meaning "common speech".
2. Mandarin is the official language (官方语言) in China.
3. 普通话 is the 官方语言 used by government officials and in education. Each region has its own dialect (方言) spoken by the local people in that area.
4. No. Chinese people who speak different dialects don't understand each other.
5. Fortunately 中国人 generally share the same writing system of 普通话, with minor variants despite the great variety of 方言.

Lesson 2 单韵母

2.1 Rhyme

鹅哥哥饿了，e e e！
大公鸡叫了，o o o！
把嘴巴张大，a a a！
阿姨的新衣，i i i！
火车快来了，u u u！
大鱼吃小鱼，ü ü ü！

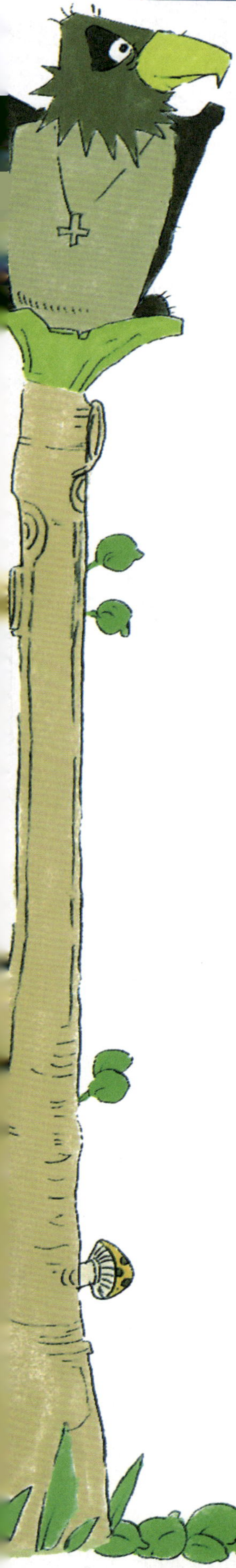

Dānyùnmǔ

É gēge è le, e e e!

Dà gōngjī jiào le, o o o!

Bǎ zuǐba zhāngdà, a a a!

Āyí de xīn yī, i i i!

Huǒchē kuài lái le, u u u!

Dà yú chī xiǎo yú, ü ü ü!

Single finals

Brother goose is hungry, e e e!
The big rooster is crowing, o o o!
Open your mouth wide, a a a!
Auntie's new clothes, i i i!
The train is coming, u u u!
The big fish is eating the small fish, ü ü ü!

单韵母 Single finals

The single finals are the main vowels.

e Let's begin with the sound of "e". This is the most frequently used English letter and most easily mispronounced because the letter is pronounced differently in other languages.

kělè 可乐

Tip: To control the openness of the mouth, relax the jaw and put one finger between your teeth and make a vowel like the sound of English short "u" as in the word "us".

o For the sound of "o", use two fingers between the teeth and round your lips like the shape of the letter "o". Make a vowel which sounds like the French word, "non".

ò 哦 ō 噢

ɑ For the sound of "ɑ", use three fingers between the teeth and open your mouth wide to pronounce "ɑ" as in the word "father".

bà 爸 mā 妈

i Let's look at "i". This time take your right index finger and place it in front of your mouth horizontally and smile ☺ when you pronounce this sound. For example, the sound of "i" is like the sound of the vowel in the word "eat". When "i" is used as a beginning sound, the spelling changes to "y" instead of "i" as in "yɑng".

i/y yīshēng 医生 yīfu 衣服

u The next sound, "u", sounds like the vowel used for the whistle of an old steam engine (woo woo!). When the "u" is used at the beginning, the spelling changes to "w" instead of "u" as in "wɑng".

u/w wūzi 屋子 wǔshù 武术

ü For the sound of "ü", pretend you are going to whistle, purse your lips, place the tongue against the back of the lower teeth and make a sound like "ü" in the German "grün".

ü/yu yǔyī 雨衣 měi yù 美玉

2.4 New words

1.	鹅	é	goose
2.	饿	è	hungry
3.	公鸡	gōngjī	rooster, cock
4.	叫	jiào	sound made by a rooster, to crow
5.	把	bǎ	*used before the object of a verb*
6.	张	zhāng	open
7.	快	kuài	soon, before long

念一念，说一说

1. Simple statement

S + V　　他　饿、渴、来、去、好、喜欢

2. Questions with 吗？　他好吗？

3. Modifiers

S + Modifier + V　　他　不 / 也 / 都 / 很　怕。

1. Is either Mandarin Chinese or English a tonal language? Or both?
2. How many tones are there in Mandarin?
3. *Pinyin* has been adopted for Mandarin; therefore, Mandarin is also an alphabetical language. True or false?
4. Is Chinese a very difficult language to learn? Explain your reasoning.

Answers:

1. Mandarin Chinese is a tonal language; English is not.
2. There are four tones（四个声调）, plus the neutral tone（轻声）in Mandarin.
3. False.
4. Linguistically speaking, 普通话 is considered to be about average level of difficulty. It seems daunting to learn how to 写 Chinese because there are so many 汉字. However, if you learn an effective way to understand the characters, it doesn't have to be that difficult. 越学越容易 yuè xué yuè róngyì! (The more you learn, the easier it becomes!) Since the adoption of the *pinyin* pronunciation system, learning to speak and read Chinese has become much easier for both Westerners and Chinese. Finally, Mandarin Chinese grammar is much easier compared to many other languages.

Lesson 3 复韵母

3.1 Rhyme

埃及有大海，ai ai ai！
妹妹有杯子，ei ei ei！
澳门有小猫，ao ao ao！
欧洲有海鸥，ou ou ou！
乌龟有尾巴，ui ui ui！
右手有牛油，iu iu iu！

Fùyùnmǔ

Āijí yǒu dà hǎi, ai ai ai!

Mèimei yǒu bēizi, ei ei ei!

Àomén yǒu xiǎo māo, ao ao ao!

Ōuzhōu yǒu hǎi'ōu, ou ou ou!

Wūguī yǒu wěiba, ui ui ui!

Yòushǒu yǒu niúyóu, iu iu iu!

Compound finals

There are big seas near Egypt, ai ai ai!

Younger sister has a cup, ei ei ei!

There are little cats in Macau, ao ao ao!

There are seagulls in Europe, ou ou ou!

Turtles have tails, ui ui ui!

There is butter on my right hand, iu iu iu!

复韵母 Compound finals

If you have already mastered the single finals, then the compound finals are a piece of cake! The only exception is the sound of "ei" as in "mèi", which is pronounced like the English word "May".

mèi — May

Compare the following sounds

e	a	o	u	
i	i		ui	iu
ei	ai	ao		ou

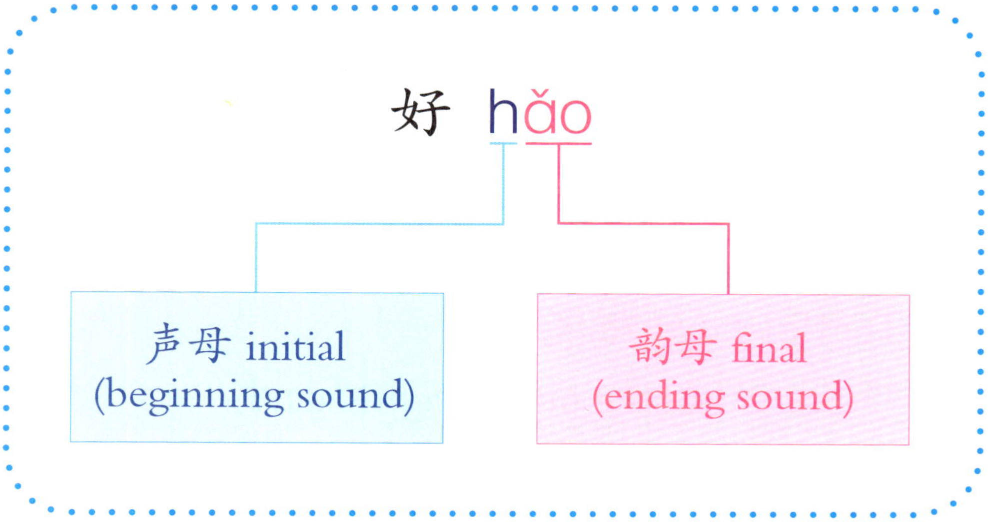

3.4 New words

1. 埃及	Āijí	Egypt
2. 海	hǎi	sea
3. 杯子	bēizi	cup
4. 澳门	Àomén	Macau
5. 欧洲	Ōuzhōu	Europe
6. 海鸥	hǎi'ōu	seagull
7. 乌龟	wūguī	turtle
8. 牛油	niúyóu	butter

涂一涂，猜一猜

Try colouring the five rings in the Olympic logo correctly. Each ring represents a continent. Can you name these five continents and guess which one is missing? Give it a try before checking the answer in the workbook.

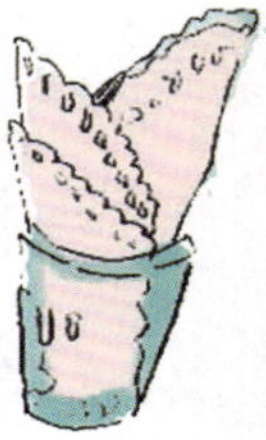

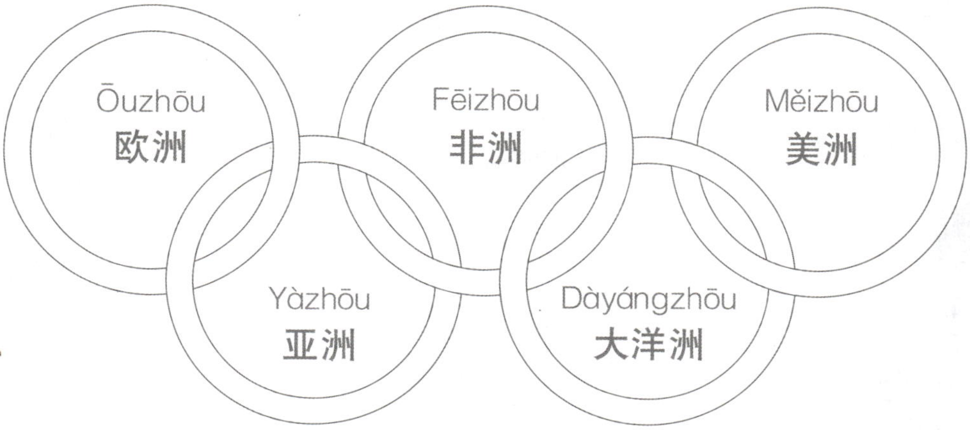

Lesson 4 结合韵（一）

4.1 Rhyme

姐姐爱爷爷，ie ie ie！

爷爷有假牙，ia ia ia！

跑跑和跳跳，iao iao iao！

苹果是水果，uo uo uo！

娃娃爱画画儿，ua ua ua！

Jiéhéyùn (Yī)

Jiějie ài yéye, ie ie ie!

Yéye yǒu jiǎyá, ia ia ia!

Pǎopao hé tiàotiao, iao iao iao!

Píngguǒ shì shuǐguǒ, uo uo uo!

Wáwa ài huà huàr, ua ua ua!

Combined finals I

Elder sister loves grandpa, ie ie ie!
Grandpa has false teeth, ia ia ia!
Running and jumping, iao iao iao!
Apple is a fruit, uo uo uo!
Babies like colouring, ua ua ua!

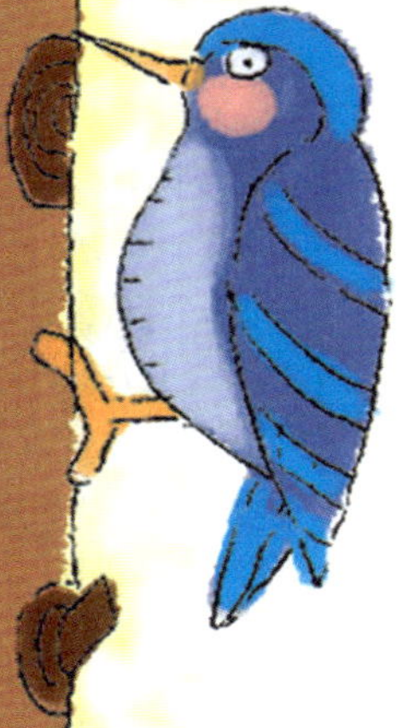

声母 Initials

There are 21 main initials in 普通话.

b p m f d t n l g k h j q x z c s zh ch sh r

The following eleven sounds are more or less the same as in English.

b	不 bù	百 bǎi	爸 bà
p	怕 pà	普 pǔ	跑 pǎo
m	门 mén	妈 mā	没 méi
f	父 fù	放 fàng	分 fēn
d	打 dǎ	地 dì	多 duō
t	他 tā	头 tóu	土 tǔ
n	男 nán	你 nǐ	那 nà
l	力 lì	老 lǎo	里 lǐ
g	个 gè	哥 gē	国 guó
k	看 kàn	口 kǒu	开 kāi
h	好 hǎo	孩 hái	很 hěn

4.4 New words

1. 爱	ài	love, like
2. 假牙	jiǎyá	false teeth
3. 娃娃	wáwa	baby, young child
4. 画画儿	huà huàr	to draw

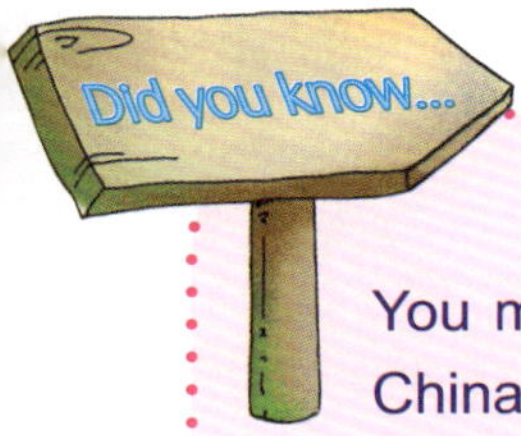

族谱 Family tree

You might wonder how the Chinese keep a record of of their "family tree". In China, the family tree is documented in a book called 族谱(zúpǔ).

Chinese attach great importance to addressing family members according to their status in the family. Therefore, in terms of defining relationships, the way they address each other is much more specific than in Western culture.

When you hear Chinese refer to a relative using "堂(táng)" as a prefix, e.g. "堂哥(tánggē)" or "堂妹(tángmèi)", you know they are referring to the father's side of the family. This group all shares the father's surname. If you hear Chinese refer to a relative using "表(biǎo)" as a prefix, e.g. "表叔(biǎoshū)" or "表妹(biǎomèi)", you know it is referring to the mother's side of the family. The surname will usually be that of the female relative's husband.

念一念，说一说

外公	外婆	爷爷	奶奶
舅舅	舅妈	爸爸	妈妈
大姨	姨父	大伯	大妈
姑姑	姑父	叔叔	婶婶
哥哥	姐姐	弟弟	妹妹
表哥	表姐	堂哥	堂姐
表弟	表妹	堂弟	堂妹

1. 叔叔是爸爸的__________。
2. 大姨是__________的姐姐。
3. 堂哥是__________的孩子。
4. 表妹是__________的孩子。
5. 爷爷、奶奶是爸爸和叔叔的__________。

Lesson 5 结合韵（二）

5.1 Rhyme

我家娃娃，爱打电话。
打给谁呀？好朋友家。

你家娃娃，喜欢画画儿。
画给谁呀？画给爸爸。

他家娃娃，喜欢种花。
送给谁呀？送给妈妈。

Jiéhéyùn (Èr)

Wǒ jiā wáwa, ài dǎ diànhuà.
Dǎ gěi shéi ya? Hǎo péngyou jiā.

Nǐ jiā wáwa, xǐhuan huà huàr.
Huà gěi shéi ya? Huà gěi bàba.

Tā jiā wáwa, xǐhuan zhòng huā.
Sòng gěi shéi ya? Sòng gěi māma.

Combined finals II

My child likes making phone calls.
-Calling to whom?
To a good friend.

Your child likes drawing.
-Drawing for whom?
Drawing for dad.

His child likes planting flowers.
-Giving to whom?
Giving to mom.

5.3 Fun time

声母 Initials

The following initials are quite different from their English pronunciation.

j q x　　z c s　　zh ch sh r

"z" sounds like "ds" in "beds"

"c" sounds like "ts" in "cats"

"s" sounds like "s" in "sun"

When followed by "h" (e.g. "zh"), simply turn the tip of your tongue up to touch the roof as "ts" in "cats" of your mouth.

"x" —There is no equivalent in English.

"r" —As the first letter of a word, it is pronounced similarly to the "r" in "rice". At the end of a word, it is pronounced similarly to the "r" in "hear".

Game: 谁吃什么？(Who is eating what?)

This is a game with two teams. The idea is for one member of each team to give one of two responses at the same time. The first team can say either "你吃 nǐ chī (you eat)" or "我吃 wǒ chī (I eat)", whilst at the same time the second team says either "鸡 jī (chicken)" or "气 qì (air)". The responses are given on the count of three. Thus, the alternatives are a combined response of "你吃鸡 nǐ chī jī (You eat chicken)", "你吃气 nǐ chī qì (You eat air)", "我吃鸡 wǒ chī jī (I eat chicken)", "我吃气 wǒ chī qì (I eat air)". When the sense of the phrase is known at the end, the winner will be obvious: the one who eats chicken. By playing these games, you will quickly master j, q and ch, after which it will be much easier for you to differentiate the other intials.

5.4 New words

1. 呀	ya	Ah! or Oh!
2. 喜欢	xǐhuan	to like
3. 种	zhòng	to plant
4. 花	huā	flower
5. 送	sòng	hand something to somebody (as a gift)

看汉字写拼音

j	jiā zhōng 家中	鸡肉	见到
q	前面	七千	上去
x	多谢	小学	现在
zh	桌子	中间	找人
ch	吃穿	橙色	睡觉
sh	水手	收拾	闪亮
r	然后	入口	儿子
z	自己	请坐	再见
c	几次	青菜	花草
s	三角	四方	几岁

Lesson 6 鼻韵母

6.1 Rhyme

缸盆碗碟，哪个深？
缸比盆深，
盆比碗深，
碗比碟深。
哪个最深？最深是缸。
哪个最浅？最浅是碟。

Bíyùnmǔ

Gāng pén wǎn dié, nǎge shēn?

Gāng bǐ pén shēn,

Pén bǐ wǎn shēn,

Wǎn bǐ dié shēn.

Nǎge zuì shēn? Zuì shēn shì gāng.

Nǎge zuì qiǎn? Zuì qiǎn shì dié.

Nasal finals

Vat, basin, bowl or plate, which is deeper?

A vat is deeper than a basin, a basin is deeper than a bowl and a bowl is deeper than a plate.

Which one is the deepest?

The deepest one is the vat.

Which one is the shallowest?

The shallowest one is the plate.

6.3 Fun time

Some rules about special letters

- A "y" is used in a syllable with " i " or " ü " at the beginning of a final.
- A "w" is used in a syllable with "u" at the beginning of a final.
- When "iou" comes after an initial, it must be written as "iu", e.g. jiū, qiū, xiū.
- When "uei" comes after an initial, it must be written as "ui", e.g. duì, cuì, guì.
- When "uen" comes after an initial, it must be written as "un", e.g. tūn, sūn, kūn.

i	yi	u	wu
ia	ya	ua	wa
iao	yao	uo	wo
ie	ye	uai	wai
iou	you	uei	wei
ian	yan	uan	wan
in	yin	uen	wen
iang	yang	uang	wang
ing	ying	ueng	weng
iong	yong		

ü	yu
üe	yue
üan	yuan
ün	yun

6.4 New words

1. 缸	gāng	vat
2. 盆	pén	basin
3. 碗	wǎn	bowl
4. 碟	dié	plate
5. 深	shēn	deep
6. 比	bǐ	compare
7. 最	zuì	most, superlatively
8. 浅	qiǎn	shallow

看汉字读拼音

		i	u	ü
an	ān xīn 安心	hòumian 后面	hǎiwān 海湾	yuán qiú 圆球
en	tāmen 他们	jīnyú 金鱼	qǐngwèn 请问	hǎoyùn 好运
ang	fàngxià 放下	liǎng ge 两个	shuāngrén 双人	
eng	péngyou 朋友	níngméng 柠檬	lǎowēng 老翁	
ong	pǔtōng 普通	yǒuyòng 有用		

Lesson 7 部件

7.1 Key words

Remembering the acronym "PARTS" will help you to relate all the key information concerning written Chinese.

Pictorial words and phonographs	xiàngxíngzì yǔ xíngshēngzì 象形字与形声字
Art of calligraphy	shūfǎ yìshù 书法艺术
Radicals and phonetic indicators	bùshǒu 部首
Traditional characters	fántǐzì 繁体字
Simplified characters	jiǎntǐzì 简体字

7.2 Pretest

Please indicate whether the statements are True or False by putting the appropriate letter in the bracket.

1. Like Egyptians, many Chinese characters began as pictures and are referred to as pictorial characters. (   )

2. Calligraphy is an art form that is highly respected by scholars as well as artists. (   )

3. The simplest writing units in Chinese writing are called units, and each unit is formed by strokes. (   )

4. As long as your Chinese character writing looks nice and neat, it is not necessary to follow a specific order of strokes for handwriting. (   )

5. Some of the more frequently used units are used as radicals. Each radical is like the word root, which gives you a clue of how it relates to the meaning. (   )

6. Most pictophonetic characters have a phonetic indicator that gives you a clue as to how the word is pronounced. (   )

Q and A

Between traditional characters and simplified characters, which are easier to learn? Why?

7.3 Fun time

关于汉字 About Chinese characters

- Many Chinese characters began as pictures. Over time they evolved into single unit characters. Single unit characters became compound unit characters through three methods:

1. combining different units, 朋 吐
2. the addition of more strokes, or 太 天
3. adding a set of strokes that form a recognizable part. 什 草

→ 肉 → 月

- In general, the simplified characters have fewer strokes, and therefore are easier to write, but sometimes harder to recognize. Traditional characters have more strokes, but are easier to recognize and more aesthetically pleasing to the eye. However, both are easy enough to learn if you learn them correctly from the start, especially with the help of increasingly advanced high-tech computer software.

甲骨文	金文	小篆	隶书	楷书（繁体）	楷书（简体）	English
門	門	門	門	門	门	door
	開	開	開	開	开	open
關	關	關	關	關	关	close

- To learn a new character easily, you should visualize it and fix it into your mind by making associations to its shape, radical, sound indicator and any other meaningful connections.

中 zhōng 种 zhǒng/zhòng 忠 zhōng 钟 zhōng 仲 zhòng
盅 zhōng 肿 zhǒng 衷 zhōng 冲 chōng 忡 chōng

★ Using a mnemonic is one of the most important keys to facilitate long-term memorization!

7.4 New words

1. 部件	bùjiàn	part, component (of a Chinese character)
2. 象形字	xiàngxíngzì	pictogram, pictorial characters
3. 形声字	xíngshēngzì	pictophonetic characters
4. 书法	shūfǎ	calligraphy
5. 艺术	yìshù	art (as an abstract concept)
6. 部首	bùshǒu	Chinese character radical
7. 繁体字	fántǐzì	traditional characters
8. 简体字	jiǎntǐzì	simplified characters

Note the differences

中国	九龙	小学	亲爱	开门
中國	九龍	小學	親愛	開門

Prepare a poster illustrating the concept of "PARTS" with examples and relevant information.

Lesson 8 二十个部首

8.1 Rhyme

金 木 水 火 土，
女 人 心 口 言，
日 月 丝 竹 草，
手 足 床 虫 辵。

钅 木 氵 灬 土
女 亻 忄 口 讠
日 月 纟 ⺮ 艹
扌 ⻊ 疒 虫 辶

Èrshí ge bùshǒu

Jīn mù shuǐ huǒ tǔ,
Nǚ rén xīn kǒu yán,
Rì yuè sī zhú cǎo,
Shǒu zú chuáng huǐ chuò.

Twenty radicals

Gold & metal, wood & tree, water & river,
fire & cooking, earth & ground,
Woman & female, man & person, heart & feelings,
mouth & opening, speech & language,
Sun & date, moon & month, silk & fabric, bamboo,
grass & plant,
Hand & player, feet & full, bed & sick,
insect & bug, distance & action.

8.3 Fun time

An efficient way to learn Chinese

Learning Chinese is fun and becomes easier if you have an efficient way — memorizing the 20 most important radicals first. Then you can expand your vocabulary to other characters effortlessly.

金 jīn: 金子 黄金	
银 yín: 白银 银行	很 hěn 跟 gēn
铜 tóng: 铜钱 铜像	洞 dòng 桐 tóng
铁 tiě: 铁路 地铁	跌 diē 迭 dié
钢 gāng: 钢丝 钢琴	刚 gāng 岗 gǎng

8.4 New words

1. 金	jīn	gold, metal
2. 木	mù	wood, tree
3. 火	huǒ	fire
4. 土	tǔ	earth, ground
5. 丝	sī	silk, fabric
6. 竹	zhú	bamboo
7. 草	cǎo	grass, plant
8. 足	zú	foot, feet
9. 床	chuáng	bed
10. 虫	chóng/huǐ	insect, bug/ the radical indicating insects and bugs

Where are 新金山 and 旧金山?

Answer: The latter is San Francisco and the former is Melbourne.

Lesson 9 新年到

9.1 Rhyme

新年到，哈哈笑，
放烟花鞭炮。
咚咚咚咚锵锵锵，
到处都热闹。
穿新衣，戴新帽，
大家吃年糕。
高高兴兴拿红包，
恭喜新年好。

新年快乐！

9.2 Pinyin & English

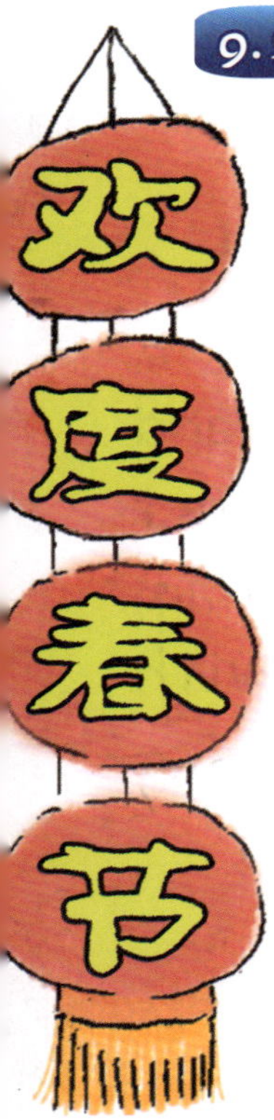

Xīnnián dào

Xīnnián dào, hāhā xiào,
Fàng yānhuā biānpào.
Dōng dōng dōng dōng qiāng qiāng qiāng,
Dàochù dōu rènao.
Chuān xīn yī, dài xīn mào,
Dàjiā chī niángāo.
Gāogāo xìngxìng ná hóngbāo,
Gōngxǐ xīnnián hǎo.
Xīnnián kuàilè!

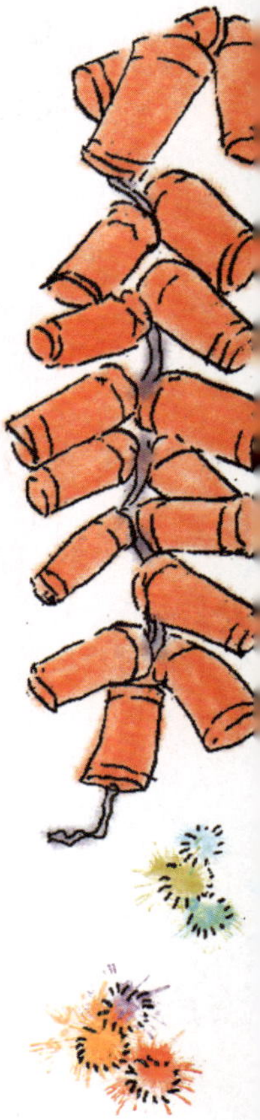

Chinese New Year is coming

Chinese New Year is coming, all the people are cheerful and laughing,
Fireworks are exploding.
Bang, bang, crash, crash, crash (sounds of drums and gongs),
Happy noises are everywhere.
Putting on new clothes and hats,
Everyone is eating New Year's cakes.
Happily receiving their red money packets,
Congratulations and Happy New Year!
Happy New Year!

9.3 Fun time

Crafts for spring festivities

What is the Chinese Zodiac animal for this year? Design and decorate your house or classroom using various Chinese art forms, e.g. calligraphy, ink painting, paper folding and cutting, New Year posters, and monthly or yearly calendars with auspicious Chinese words on red paper. Have fun practicing calligraphy!

9.4 New words

1.	哈哈	hāhā	*sound of laughing*
2.	笑	xiào	laugh
3.	放	fàng	set off (fireworks)
4.	烟花	yānhuā	fireworks
5.	鞭炮	biānpào	firecracker
6.	咚	dōng	*sound of beating a drum*
7.	锵	qiāng	*sound of gong clanking*
8.	到处	dàochù	everywhere, all over
9.	热闹	rènao	bustling with noise and excitement, lively
10.	戴	dài	put on
11.	帽	mào	hat
12.	年糕	niángāo	New Year's cake
13.	红包	hóngbāo	red packet, lucky money given as a gift

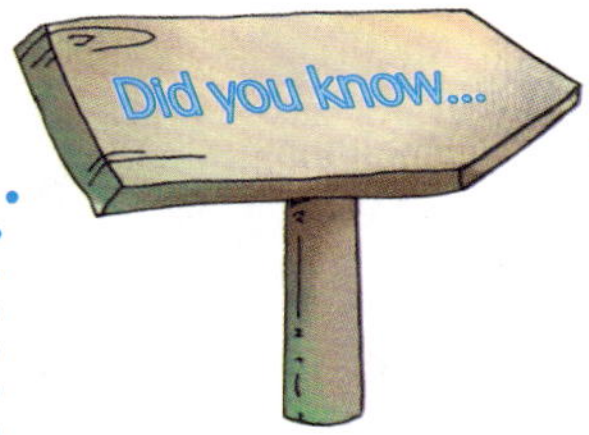

中国新年 Chinese New Year

新年 is also referred to as 春节, 过年 (celebrate Chinese New Year) or 旧历年 (lunar New Year). Some people think that Chinese New Year is more like Christmas in the West. Some think it's more like Thanksgiving. Explain what you think and give reasons.

Lesson 10 端午节

10.1 Rhyme

五月五，端午节，
纪念屈原。
吃粽子，挂香袋，
看看龙船比赛。

Duānwǔ Jié

Wǔyuè wǔ, Duānwǔ Jié,
Jìniàn Qū Yuán.
Chī zòngzi, guà xiāng dài,
Kànkan lóngchuán bǐsài.

Dragon Boat Festival

The Fifth of May (the lunar calendar),
Dragon Boat Festival,
In honour of the great poet—Qu Yuan.
Eat steamed rice dumplings and wear
fragrant pouches,
Watch dragon boat races.

10.3 Fun time

做端午彩粽

Food plays an important part in all kinds of traditional festivities. The special food associated with 端午节 is delicious 粽子 wrapped in bamboo leaves. There are also delicate fragrant pouches or sachets imitating the shape of 粽子. They can be made as decorative items or as special gifts for loved ones. Try it yourself!

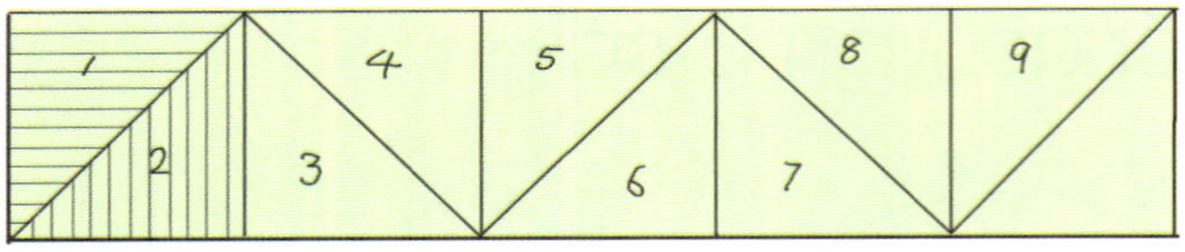

Steps:

1. Take a piece of heavy duty recycled paper 3 cm x 15 cm in size.
2. Fold it into nine continuous triangles as illustrated.
3. Wrap sections 1–4 to shape a lower cup and sections 5–6 as an upper covering to form a dumpling. Leave some fragrant dry herbs or perfumed cotton inside before continuing wrapping 2 more sections, then tuck the last part into the gap.
4. Use colourful thread beginning at either the top or bottom and weave it along the edge lines until all sides are covered.
5. Make a knot on a thread before pulling it through the dumpling to the bottom and decorate it with a tassel.

10.4 New words

1. 端午节	Duānwǔ Jié	Dragon Boat Festival
2. 五月	wǔyuè	May (lit. the 5th month)
3. 纪念	jìniàn	commemorate or memorialize
4. 屈原	Qū Yuán	Qu Yuan (name of a great poet)
5. 粽子	zòngzi	sticky rice dumpling usually wrapped in bamboo leaves
6. 香袋	xiāng dài	fragrant bag, sachet
7. 龙船	lóngchuán	dragon boat
8. 比赛	bǐsài	race, competition

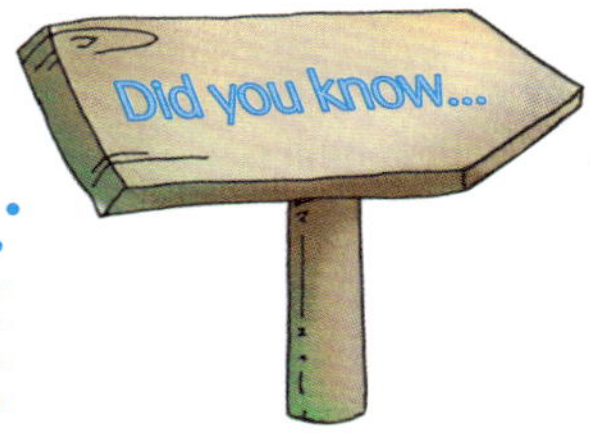

端午节 Dragon Boat Festival

端午节 is also referred to as 五月节 or 诗人节 (the Poet's Day). It is not only celebrated as a traditional Chinese festival, dragon boat races have also become a popular international sporting event.

允文允武 (yǔn wén yǔn wǔ) or 文武兼备 (wénwǔ jiānbèi) means to be well-versed both in literary writing and martial arts.

Lesson 11 中秋节

11.1 Rhyme

八月十五中秋节，
大家都来赏月亮。
月宫嫦娥，玉兔相伴，
吴刚伐桂，说不完。

庆祝中秋，庆祝中秋，
尝尝月饼，赏月亮。
高挂天上，又圆又亮，
照遍大地，照海洋。

11.2 Pinyin & English

Zhōngqiū Jié

Bāyuè shíwǔ Zhōngqiū Jié,
Dàjiā dōu lái shǎng yuèliang.
Yuègōng Cháng'é, yùtù xiāng bàn,
Wú Gāng fá guì, shuō bu wán.

Qìngzhù Zhōngqiū, qìngzhù Zhōngqiū,
Chángchang yuèbing, shǎng yuèliang.
Gāo guà tiānshang, yòu yuán yòu liàng,
Zhàobiàn dàdì, zhào hǎiyáng.

Mid-Autumn Festival

August 15th of the lunar calendar is the Mid-Autumn Festival.
People are all going outside to enjoy the moon.
Chang'e is said to be in the Moon Palace and accompanied by Jade Rabbit,
Wu Gang is said to be cutting the ever-growing laurel , and so on...

Celebrating the Mid-Autumn Festival, celebrating the Mid-Autumn Festival,
Tasting the mooncakes and enjoying the moonlight.
High up in the sky, the moon is brightly shining,
Shining all over the land and on the ocean.

做中秋立体卡片

Make a simple pop-up lantern with your own drawing and decorate the border with patterns in Chinese characters.

1. Fold a half sheet of A4 or letter size paper in the middle and cut out a symmetrical lantern.
2. Draw a design on it.
3. Decorate an A4 size background card.
4. Apply the glue on the shaded section. Attach the lantern to the background card.
5. Be sure to leave enough space so it can pop up.

① Cut out
② Draw
③ Design
④ Apply glue
⑤ Attach the design to the background

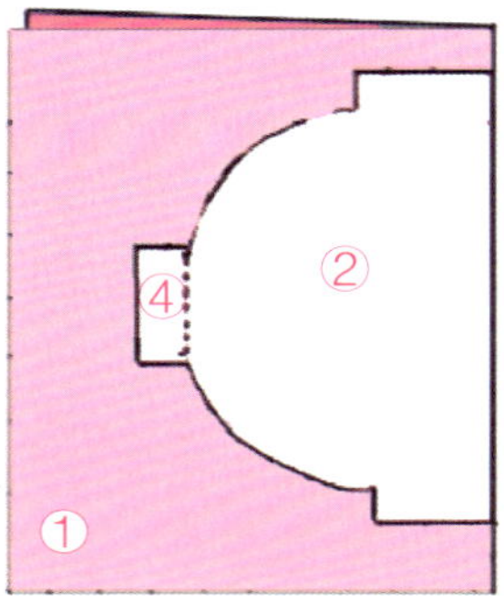

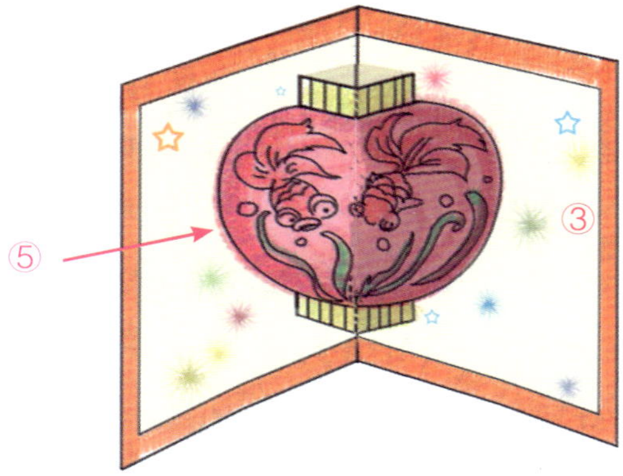

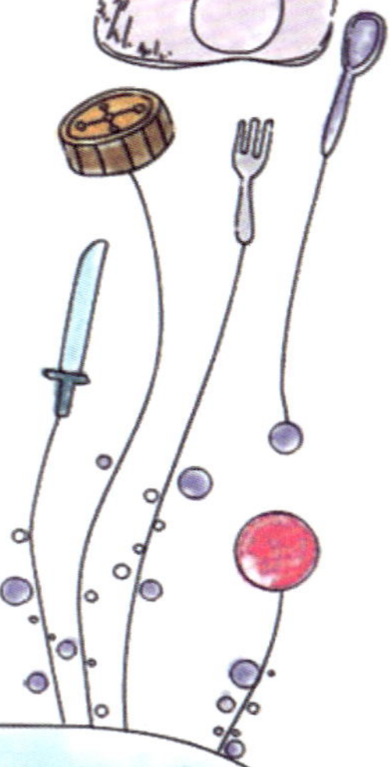

11.4 New words

1. 中秋节	Zhōngqiū Jié	Mid-Autumn Festival
2. 八月	bāyuè	August (lit. the 8th month)
3. 赏	shǎng	enjoy, appreciate
4. 月亮	yuèliang	moon
5. 月宫	yuègōng	Moon Palace
6. 嫦娥	Cháng'é	Chang'e, goddess of the moon
7. 玉兔	yùtù	Jade Rabbit
8. 相伴	xiāng bàn	companion, keep somebody company
9. 吴刚	Wú Gāng	Wu Gang (name of a person)
10. 伐	fá	to cut
11. 桂	guì	cassia-bark tree, osmanthus, laurel
12. 庆祝	qìngzhù	celebrate
13. 月饼	yuèbing	mooncake
14. 照	zhào	shine
15. 大地	dàdì	earth, land
16. 海洋	hǎiyáng	ocean

Did you know...

中秋节 Mid-Autumn Festival

中秋节 is also referred to as 八月节. Have you heard all the stories about 中秋节? For example, about the goddess of the moon 嫦娥, the Jade Rabbit 玉兔, the man 吴刚 cutting the ever-growing laurel, the mooncake (月饼), or the old man under the moon 月下老人 (matchmaker)?

Go to a website or library for more information on them and tell your class which story you like the most and why.

Lesson 12 爱护动物

12.1 Rhyme

我很喜欢小乌龟，
小乌龟，小乌龟。
我很喜欢小乌龟。
你喜欢什么动物？

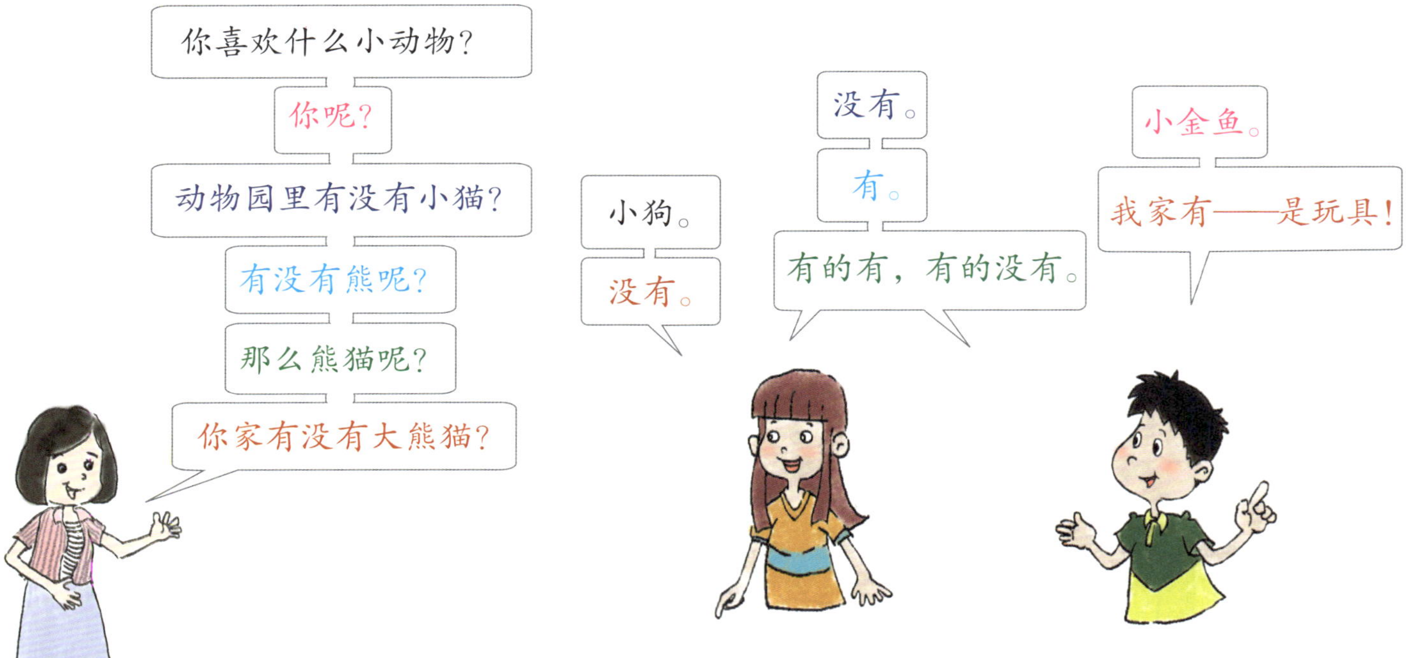

我们喜欢小动物，
小动物，小动物。
我们喜欢小动物，
人人爱护小动物。

12.2 Pinyin & English

Àihù dòngwù

Wǒ hěn xǐhuan xiǎo wūguī,
Xiǎo wūguī, xiǎo wūguī.
Wǒ hěn xǐhuan xiǎo wūguī.
Nǐ xǐhuan shénme dòngwù?

Nǐ xǐhuan shénme xiǎo dòngwù?
–Xiǎo gǒu.
Nǐ ne?
–Xiǎo jīnyú.
Dòngwùyuán li yǒu méiyǒu xiǎo māo?
–Méiyǒu.
Yǒu méiyǒu xióng ne?
–Yǒu.
Nàme xióngmāo ne?
–Yǒude yǒu, yǒude méiyǒu.
Nǐ jiā yǒu méiyǒu dà xióngmāo?
–Méiyǒu.
–Wǒ jiā yǒu —— shì wánjù!

Wǒmen xǐhuan xiǎo dòngwù,
Xiǎo dòngwù, xiǎo dòngwù.
Wǒmen xǐhuan xiǎo dòngwù,
Rénrén àihù xiǎo dòngwù.

We like animals

I like little turtles very much,
Little turtles, little turtles.
I like little turtles very much.
What animal do you like?

What small animal do you like?
- I like puppies.
How about you?
- I like small goldfish.
Are there any cats in the zoo?
- No.
What about bears?
- Yes.
Are there any giant pandas in the zoo?
-Some zoos keep them, some don't.
Do you have a giant panda at home?
- No, I don't.
- Yes, I have one. It's a toy!

We like small animals,
Small animals, small animals.
We like small animals,
Everyone takes care of small animals.

12.3 Fun time

Grammar point

Word order is an important grammatical means in Chinese. The same words with different orders indicate different meanings.

书包	schoolbag	包书	wrap up the book
火山	volcano	山火	hill fire
饭盒	lunch box	盒饭	packed meal
鸡蛋	hen's egg	蛋鸡	laying hen

A beautiful mistake

猫熊 is more correct for the panda according to the grammar. However, common usage has made it 熊猫. In written Chinese characters, other than 4 dots (灬) representing the 4 legs of animals and the side dog radical (犭), there are some more common radicals that refer to animals in modern Chinese characters, e.g.

虫 鱼 鸟 牛 羊 马 犬 豕

12.4 New words

1. 爱护	àihù	treat with care and kindness
2. 动物	dòngwù	animal
3. 狗	gǒu	dog
4. 动物园	dòngwùyuán	zoo (lit. animal park)
5. 熊	xióng	bear
6. 熊猫	xióngmāo	panda
7. 玩具	wánjù	toy

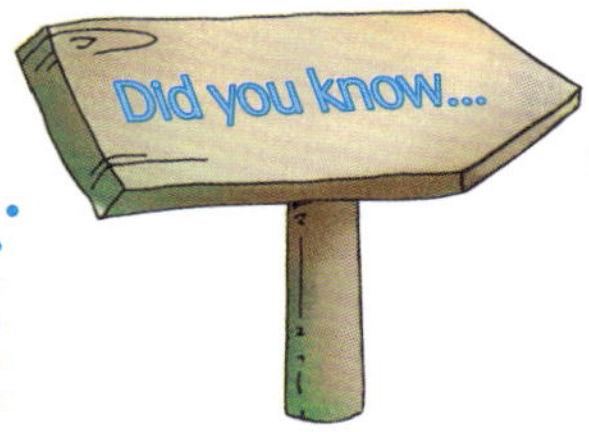

福娃 Lucky Children

What is the favorite animal in China nowadays? What the popular and rare animals were also among the 2008 Olympic mascots (福娃 lit. Lucky Children)?

Lesson 13 阿里山上

13.1 Rhyme

一二三，到台湾，
台湾有个阿里山。
阿里山上有神木，
明年一起去大陆。

Ālǐ Shān shang

Yī èr sān, dào Táiwān,

Táiwān yǒu ge Ālǐ Shān.

Ālǐ Shān shang yǒu shén mù,

Míngnián yìqǐ qù dàlù.

On Mt. Ali

One, two, three, arrive in Taiwan.
In Taiwan stands Mt. Ali.
On Mt. Ali there's a sacred tree.
Next year, let's go together to
China's mainland.

Grammar point

The time aspect usually precedes the location, and may appear at the beginning of a sentence, or after a subject.

	Time	Subject	Location	Verb
Present	现在	他	在美国	开会。
Past	昨天	我	去学校	上课了。
Future	明天	哥哥	去图书馆	看书。

	Subject	Time	Location	Verb
Present	他	现在	在中国	学习。
Past	老师	中秋节	去日本	玩儿了。
Future	哥哥	明天	去书店	买书。

Interesting radicals

There are other common radicals besides 木，米，竹，瓜，豆... that refer to plants in modern Chinese characters.

Some radicals are used more than once in the same character to form a new，but often related character，such as

木　林（lín）　森（sēn）
日　昌（chāng）　晶（jīng）
口　吕（lǚ）　品（pǐn）
火　炎（yán）
水　淼（miǎo）

13.4 New words

1. 阿里山	Ālǐ Shān	a famous mountain in central Taiwan, China
2. 神	shén	god or deity
3. 神木	shén mù	sacred tree
4. 明年	míngnián	next year
5. 大陆	dàlù	China's mainland

猜一猜

Have you wondered why 今 as in 今天 sounds the same as 金 as in 黄金? What about 明 as in 明天?

Answers:
今天 — Today is as precious as gold! 明天 — An optimist is always looking forward to a brighter tomorrow.

Lesson 14 书包不见了

14.1 Rhyme

哎呀！怎么书包不见了？
怎么书包不见了？
没带午饭和运动服，
没有本子和文具袋。
书包不见不能上学，
怎么好？

哎呀！怎么书包不见了？
怎么书包不见了？
没有手机打电话，
没有钞票，也没车票。
书包不见不能回家，
怎么好？

哈哈！我的书包找到了！
我的书包找到了！
里面有手机能打电话，
还有钞票，也有车票。
有了车票可以回家，
多么好！

14.2 Pinyin & English

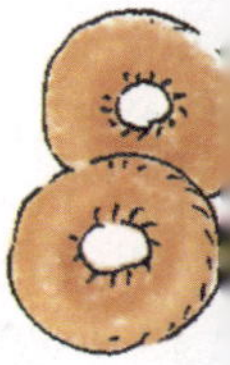

Shūbāo bújiàn le

Āiyā! Zěnme shūbāo bújiàn le?
Zěnme shūbāo bújiàn le?
Méi dài wǔfàn hé yùndòngfú,
Méiyǒu běnzi hé wénjùdài.
Shūbāo bújiàn bù néng shàng xué,
Zěnme hǎo?

Āiyā! Zěnme shūbāo bújiàn le?
Zěnme shūbāo bújiàn le?
Méiyǒu shǒujī dǎ diànhuà,
Méiyǒu chāopiào, yě méi chēpiào.
Shūbāo bújiàn bù néng huí jiā,
Zěnme hǎo?

Hāhā! Wǒ de shūbāo zhǎodào le!
Wǒ de shūbāo zhǎodào le!
Lǐmian yǒu shǒujī néng dǎ diànhuà,
Hái yǒu chāopiào, yě yǒu chēpiào.
Yǒule chēpiào kěyǐ huí jiā,
Duōme hǎo!

My schoolbag has gone

Oh no! Where is my schoolbag?
Where is my schoolbag?
I didn't bring my lunch box nor sportswear.
I have not notebooks nor a pencil case.
I can't go to school without my schoolbag.
What shall I do?

Oh no! Where is my schoolbag?
Where is my schoolbag?
I have not my mobile phone to make calls.
I have not money nor a travel ticket.
I can't go home without my schoolbag .
What shall I do?

Yeah! I found my schoolbag.
I found my schoolbag.
Inside there is my mobile phone, money and travel ticket.
How wonderful that I can go home now!

14.3 Fun time

比一比

没有/没/不

没有 （+ N） = have not

没 （+ V） = did not

不 （+ V） = do not

念一念，说一说

1. 包 is followed or preceded by another word.

包子 包饭 包机 包车 包公 包心菜 包圆儿

面包 书包 背包 打包 皮包 腰包 沙包

草包 邮包 手提包 急救包 蒙古包

2. 怎么……？什么……？

多么 + Adj.!

为什么……？因为……。

14.4 New words

1. 哎呀	āiyā	Oh no!
2. 不见	bújiàn	disappear, be gone
3. 带	dài	bring
4. 午饭	wǔfàn	lunch
5. 运动服	yùndòngfú	sportswear
6. 本子	běnzi	notebook
7. 文具袋	wénjùdài	pencil case
8. 不能	bù néng	cannot, be unable to
9. 怎么好	zěnme hǎo	What shall I do?
10. 上学	shàng xué	go to school
11. 手机	shǒujī	mobile phone (lit. hand phone)
12. 钞票	chāopiào	bank note, paper money
13. 车票	chēpiào	ticket for land travel
14. 回家	huí jiā	return home, go home
15. 找到	zhǎodào	find (something missing)
16. 还有	hái yǒu	and, additionally
17. 多么	duōme	how + adj.

你的书包里有什么？

如果书包不见了，你会怎么样？

怎么避免（bìmiǎn，avoid）呢？

Lesson 15 数到十

15.1 Rhyme

数到一，请爸爸给我一支笔。

数到二，请妈妈教我唱儿歌。

数到三，请爷爷陪我去爬山。

数到四，请奶奶带我逛公司。

数到五，叔叔阿姨爱跳舞。

数到六，大哥大姐爱打球。

数到七，小弟弟会说对不起。

数到八，小妹妹喜欢打电话。

数到九，小朋友会分左和右。

数到十，我们会从一数到十。

15.2 Pinyin & English

Shǔdào shí

Shǔdào yī, qǐng bàba gěi wǒ yì zhī bǐ.

Shǔdào èr, qǐng māma jiāo wǒ chàng érgē.

Shǔdào sān, qǐng yéye péi wǒ qù pá shān.

Shǔdào sì, qǐng nǎinai dài wǒ guàng gōngsī.

Shǔdào wǔ, shūshu āyí ài tiào wǔ.

Shǔdào liù, dàgē dàjiě ài dǎ qiú.

Shǔdào qī, xiǎodìdi huì shuō duìbuqǐ.

Shǔdào bā, xiǎomèimei xǐhuan dǎ diànhuà.

Shǔdào jiǔ, xiǎopéngyǒu huì fēn zuǒ hé yòu.

Shǔdào shí, wǒmen huì cóng yī shǔ dào shí.

Count to 10

Count to 1, I ask dad for a pen.

Count to 2, I ask mom to teach me to sing.

Count to 3, I ask grandpa to go hiking with me.

Count to 4, I ask grandma to take me shopping.

Count to 5, my uncle and aunt like dancing.

Count to 6, my elder brother and elder sister like playing ball games.

Count to 7, my little younger brother understands when to say "I'm sorry".

Count to 8, my little younger sister likes making phone calls.

Count to 9, the children can tell their left from their right.

Count to 10, we can count from 1 to 10.

15.3 Fun time

念一念，说一说

Time	从一点到三点	从早到晚
Space	从这里到那里	从里到外
Somebody	从大人到小孩	从老师到学生
Something	从吃的到喝的	从头上的帽子 到脚上的鞋子

写一写

1. 比千和万多的数字

____

2. 第一、第二、第三……

____

3. 从……到……

____

15.4 New words

1. 教	jiāo	teach
2. 陪	péi	accompany
3. 打球	dǎ qiú	play a ball game
4. 分	fēn	tell one from another, divide
5. 从…到…	cóng…dào…	from… to…

自己写儿歌

数到一，______________________________。

__________，______________________________。

__________，______________________________。

__________，______________________________。

__________，______________________________。

__________，______________________________。

__________，______________________________。

__________，______________________________。

__________，______________________________。

__________，______________________________。

Lesson 16 买东西

16.1 Rhyme

多少？多少？一共多少钱？
太贵，太贵，还是太贵了！
便宜点儿，便宜点儿，再便宜点儿！

找钱，找钱，请找我钱！
快点儿，快点儿，请快一点儿！

请给我这个，请给他那个。
请给我老师一杯热水，
请给我朋友一杯冰水，好吗？

16.2 Pinyin & English

Mǎi dōngxi

Duōshao? Duōshao? Yígòng duōshao qián?
Tài guì, tài guì, háishi tài guì le!
Piányi diǎnr, piányi diǎnr, zài piányi diǎnr!

Zhǎo qián, zhǎo qián, qǐng zhǎo wǒ qián!
Kuài diǎnr, kuài diǎnr, qǐng kuài yìdiǎnr!

Qǐng gěi wǒ zhège, qǐng gěi tā nàge.
Qǐng gěi wǒ lǎoshī yì bēi rè shuǐ,
Qǐng gěi wǒ péngyou yì bēi bīng shuǐ, hǎo ma?

Going shopping

How much? How much? Altogether how much?
Too much! Too much! Still too much!
Cheaper! Cheaper! Make it even cheaper.

Get change! Get change! Please give my change.
Hurry up! Hurry up! Please hurry up!

Please give me this. Please give him that.
Would you please give a cup of hot water to my teacher, and a glass of ice water to my friend?

16.3 Fun time

货币 Currencies

Can you name the following major currencies?

16.4 New words

1. 买	mǎi	buy
2. 贵	guì	expensive, costly
3. 便宜	piányi	cheap, inexpensive
4. 找钱	zhǎo qián	give change
5. 杯	bēi	*a measure word*
6. 冰	bīng	ice

These words are both easy and extremely practical!

想一想，写一写，你在哪里会用到？

请快一点儿！________________

慢点儿！________________

小心点儿！________________

大声点儿！________________

小声点儿！________________

写写反义词

多 — 少	贵 —	快 —	热 —

Lesson 17 别生气

17.1 Rhyme

小姐，小姐，别生气，
明天请你去看戏。
我坐椅子你坐地，
我吃香蕉你吃皮。

小姐，小姐，别生气，
明天请你去看戏。
你坐椅子我坐地，
你吃香蕉我吃皮。

17.2 Pinyin & English

Bié shēng qì

Xiǎojiě, xiǎojiě, bié shēng qì,
Míngtiān qǐng nǐ qù kàn xì.
Wǒ zuò yǐzi nǐ zuò dì,
Wǒ chī xiāngjiāo nǐ chī pí.

Xiǎojiě, xiǎojiě, bié shēng qì,
Míngtiān qǐng nǐ qù kàn xì.
Nǐ zuò yǐzi wǒ zuò dì,
Nǐ chī xiāngjiāo wǒ chī pí.

Don't get angry

Young lady, young lady, don't get angry.
Tomorrow I'll take you to the show.
I'll sit on a chair and you'll sit on the ground.
I'll eat the banana and you'll eat the peel!

Young lady, young lady, don't get angry.
Tomorrow I'll take you to the show.
You'll sit on a chair and I'll sit on the ground.
You'll eat the banana and I'll eat the peel!

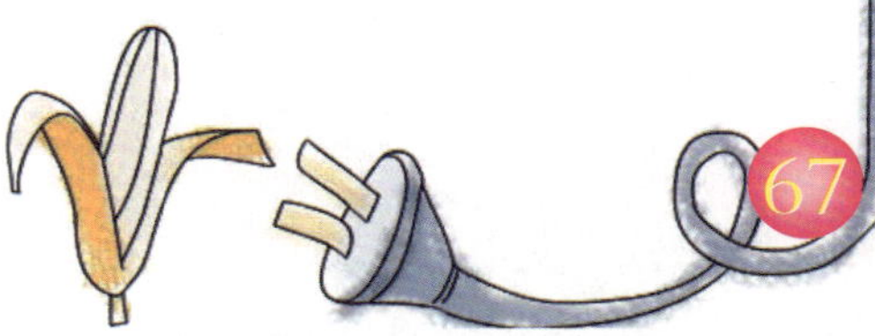

17.3 Fun time

Words to convey feelings

开心　快乐　高兴

不开心　不快乐　不高兴

生气　伤心　难过

Addressing people appropriately

王老师　李师傅

张先生　张叔叔　张太太

谢小姐　谢阿姨

大姐　大哥

17.4 New words

1. 生气	shēng qì	get angry
2. 小姐	xiǎojiě	young lady, Miss
3. 明天	míngtiān	tomorrow
4. 请	qǐng	ask somebody to do something, invite
5. 看戏	kàn xì	watch a show or play
6. 地	dì	ground
7. 皮	pí	skin, peel

念一念，说一说

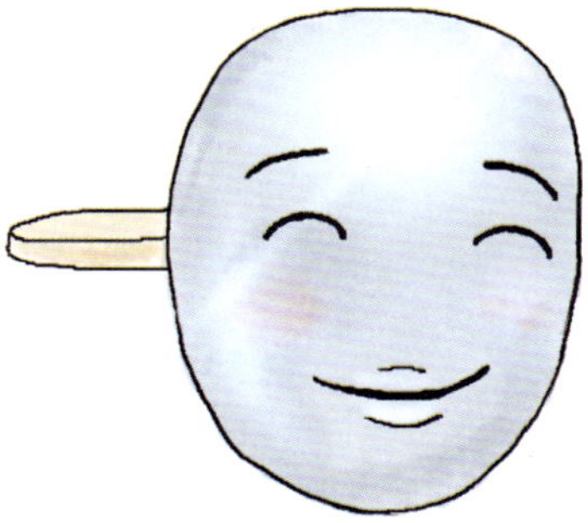

xiào
笑

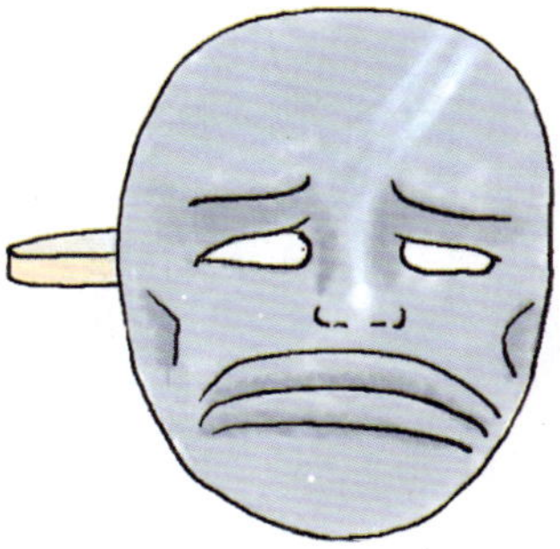

kū
哭

大笑	dàxiào	笑声	xiàoshēng	哭哭啼啼	kūkutítí
好笑	hǎoxiào	说笑	shuōxiào	哭泣	kūqì
欢笑	huānxiào	可笑	kěxiào	大哭	dà kū
笑话	xiàohua	冷笑	lěngxiào	痛哭	tòngkū
笑嘻嘻	xiàoxīxī	开玩笑	kāi wánxiào	哭了	kū le

Lesson 18 三轮车

18.1 Rhyme

三轮车，跑得快，
上面坐位老奶奶，
要九十块，给一百。
你说奇怪不奇怪？

不奇怪，不奇怪，
多给十块不算多，
少给十块不慷慨！

小猴子，吱吱叫，
肚子饿了不能跳。
给香蕉，还不要，
你说好笑不好笑？

Sānlúnchē

Sānlúnchē, pǎo de kuài,
Shàngmian zuò wèi lǎonǎinai,
Yào jiǔshí kuài, gěi yìbǎi.
Nǐ shuō qíguài bu qíguài?

Bù qíguài, bù qíguài,
Duō gěi shí kuài bú suàn duō,
Shǎo gěi shí kuài bu kāngkǎi!

Xiǎo hóuzi, zhīzhī jiào,
Dùzi è le bù néng tiào.
Gěi xiāngjiāo, hái bú yào,
Nǐ shuō hǎoxiào bu hǎoxiào?

The rickshaw

The rickshaw is moving so fast!
An old lady is sitting on the seat.
90 dollars she must pay,
She gave one hundred instead.
Now I ask, isn't that strange?

Not at all, not at all,
10 dollars more is not a lot,
10 dollars less would not be
generous enough!

Little monkey is crying "eeh, eeh",
He cannot jump when he's hungry.
Bananas were given to him,
But surprisingly he's not interested.
Now don't you think that's funny?

18.3 Fun time

比一比

Compare the first stanza of this more than 50 year old version of the song with the new version. Note and explain the differences.

三轮车，跑得快，
上面坐个老太太，
要五毛，给一块。
你说奇怪不奇怪？

Hint:

1. Measure words
2. Salutation
3. Money

三轮车 is also called 人力车 which literarily means "human powered vehicle".

Answers: Measure word 位/个; Salutation 老奶奶/老太太; Money 九十，一百/五毛，一块.

18.4 New words

1. 三轮车	sānlúnchē	rickshaw
2. 位	wèi	*a polite measure word for people*
3. 老奶奶	lǎonǎinai	old lady, grandma
4. 不算	bú suàn	not considered
5. 慷慨	kāngkǎi	generous
6. 猴子	hóuzi	monkey
7. 吱吱	zhīzhī	eeh, eeh (*sound a monkey makes*)
8. 肚子	dùzi	belly, stomach
9. 跳	tiào	jump
10. 好笑	hǎoxiào	funny

念一念，说一说

坐车　坐船　坐飞机
搭车　搭船　搭机
骑单车　骑自行车
开车　驾车
赶车　赶牛车　赶马车

他天天走路上学。
哥哥骑车上学。
爸爸妈妈坐车上班。
星期天开车出去玩儿。

Lesson 19 中国地名

19.1 Rhyme

长江黄河各三两，两岛两山两湖广。
五个民族自治区，京津沪渝加澳港。
东北三省云海川，福贵甘甜陕平安。

江苏，浙江，江西，河南，河北；
台湾岛，海南岛，山东，山西，湖南，湖北，广东，广西；
新疆维吾尔自治区，内蒙古自治区，宁夏回族自治区，
西藏自治区，广西壮族自治区；
北京，天津，上海，重庆，澳门，香港；
辽宁，吉林，黑龙江，云南，青海，四川；
福建，贵州，甘肃，陕西，安徽。

Zhōngguó dìmíng

Cháng Jiāng Huáng Hé gè sān liǎng,
Liǎng dǎo liǎng shān liǎng Hú Guǎng.
Wǔ ge mínzú zìzhìqū,
Jīng Jīn Hù Yú jiā Ào Gǎng.
Dōngběi sān shěng Yún Hǎi Chuān,
Fú Guì gāntián Shǎn píng'ān.

Place names of China

The Yangtze River has three adjoining provinces,
while the Yellow River has two.
Two "islands", two "mountains", two *Hu* and two *Guang*.
Five autonomous regions, Beijing, Tianjin,
Shanghai, Chongqing, plus Macau & Hong Kong.
There are three northeast provinces, plus
Yun, Hai, Chuan,
Fu, Gui, Gan, Shan and An.

19.3 Fun time

Geography

Study the map of China and learn the proper name of each place including municipalities, provinces, autonomous regions, and special administrative regions.

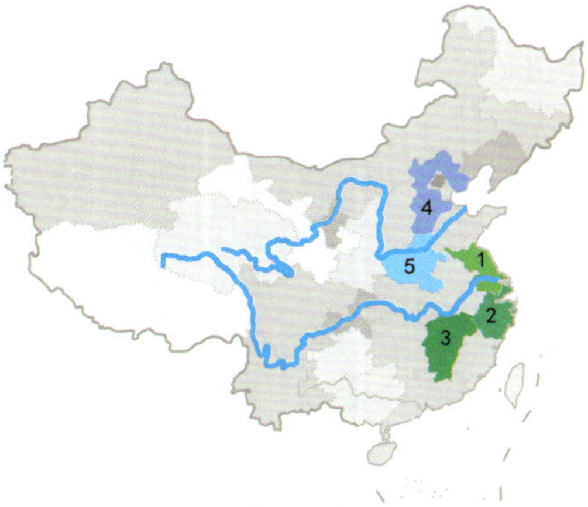

长江黄河各三两

1.江苏 2.浙江 3.江西
4.河北 5.河南

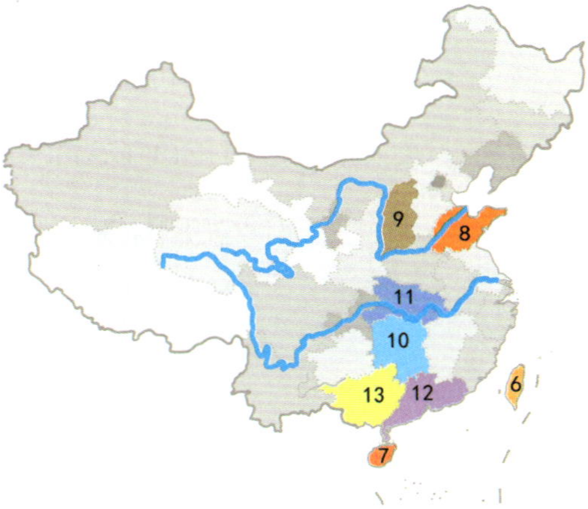

两岛两山两湖广

6.台湾岛 7.海南岛 8.山东 9.山西
10.湖南 11.湖北 12.广东 13.广西

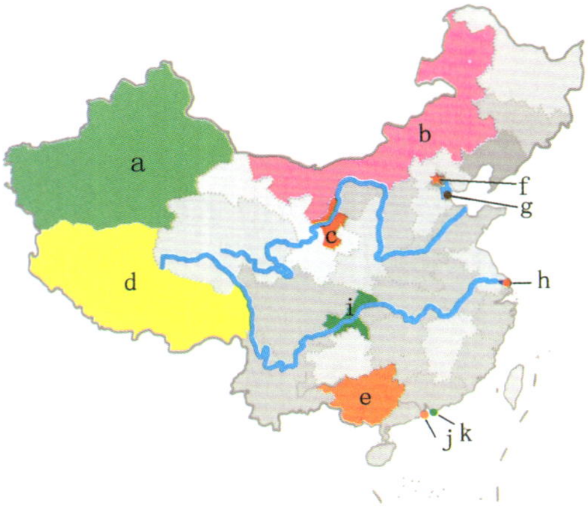

五个民族自治区

a.新疆维吾尔自治区 b.内蒙古自治区
c.宁夏回族自治区 d.西藏自治区
e.广西壮族自治区

京津沪渝加澳港

f.北京 g.天津 h.上海 i.重庆
j.澳门 k.香港

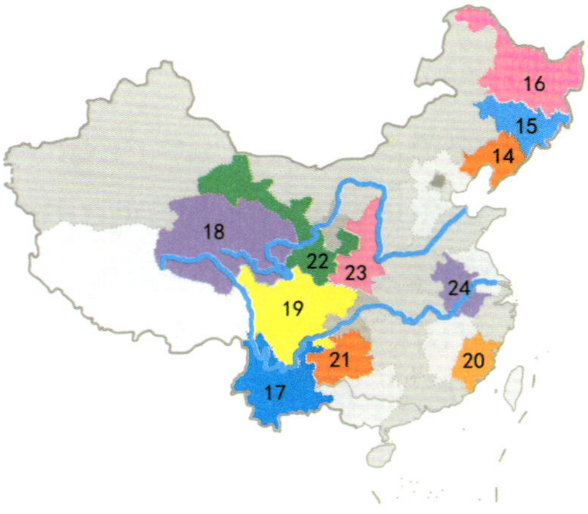

东北三省云海川

14.辽宁 15.吉林 16.黑龙江
17.云南 18.青海 19.四川

福贵甘甜陕平安

20.福建 21.贵州 22.甘肃
23.陕西 24.安徽

19.4 New words

1. 长江	Cháng Jiāng	Yangtze River
2. 黄河	Huáng Hé	Yellow River
3. 各	gè	each
4. 岛	dǎo	island
5. 湖	Hú	*Hu* (the first character of the name of the two provinces, 湖北 and 湖南)
6. 广	Guǎng	*Guang* (the first character of the name of the two provinces, 广东 and 广西)
7. 民族	mínzú	ethnic group
8. 自治区	zìzhìqū	autonomous region
9. 京	Jīng	abbreviation for Beijing
10. 津	Jīn	abbreviation for Tianjin
11. 沪	Hù	abbreviation for Shanghai
12. 渝	Yú	abbreviation for Chongqing
13. 加	jiā	plus, add
14. 澳	Ào	abbreviation for Macau
15. 港	Gǎng	abbreviation for Hong Kong
16. 东北	Dōngběi	Northeast (area of China)
17. 省	shěng	province
18. 云	Yún	abbreviation for Yunnan Province (lit. cloud)
19. 川	Chuān	abbreviation for Sichuan Province (lit. river)
20. 福	Fú	abbreviation for Fujian Province (lit. luck, blessing)
21. 贵	Guì	abbreviation for Guizhou Province (lit. honour, noble, precious)
22. 甘	Gān	abbreviation for Gansu Province (lit. sweet, pleasant, willingly)
23. 陕	Shǎn	abbreviation for Shaanxi Province (lit. narrow path)
24. 平安	píng'ān	peace, peaceful

An English crossword puzzle

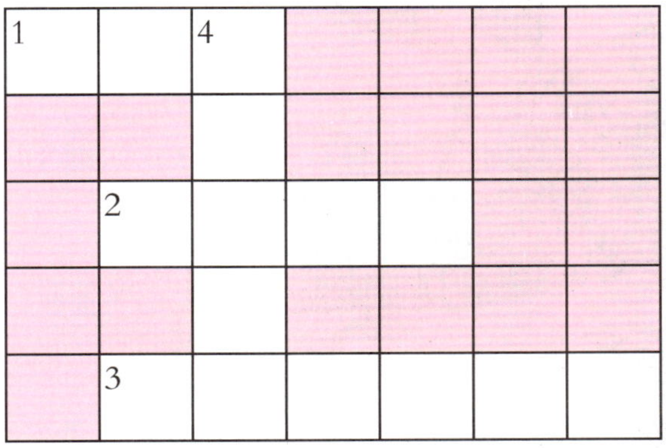

Across:

1. The 3-letter abbreviation for China
2. The 4-letter prefix which comes from Latin meaning China
3. The 6-letter word that Russians used to refer to China

Down:

4. The 5-letter word for the Middle Kingdom

Answers: 1.PRC, 2.Sino, 3.Cathay, 4.China

Lesson 20 中国朝代

20.1 Rhyme

唐尧虞舜夏商周，
春秋战国乱悠悠。
秦汉三国晋统有，
南朝北朝是对头。
隋唐五代又十国，
宋元明清帝王休。

Zhōngguó cháodài

Tángyáo Yúshùn Xià Shāng Zhōu,
Chūnqiū Zhànguó luànyōuyōu.

Qín Hàn Sānguó Jìn tǒngyǒu,
Náncháo Běicháo shì duìtou.

Suí Táng Wǔdài yòu Shíguó,
Sòng Yuán Míng Qīng dìwáng xiū.

Chinese dynasties

Tangyao, Yushun, Xia, Shang, Zhou,
From the Spring-Autumn to Warring States there was chaos.

Jin united the whole nation after Qin, Han and the Three Kingdoms.
The Southern and Northern dynasties were in opposition to each other.

After Sui and Tang there were Five Dynasties and Ten Kingdoms.
After the Song, Yuan, Ming and Qing dynasties, monarchic rule came to an end.

20.3 Fun time

Qin and Qing vs. Chin and Ching

The *pinyin* "Qinchao" in an earlier Romanization was spelled "Chinchao". The *pinyin* "Qing" as in "Qingchao" was formerly spelled "Chingchao". "Qinchao" was the first united nation in Chinese history. It is pronounced using the second tone, which is a rising tone like a rising star. The last dynasty was "Qingchao", using the first tone like a heart monitor after the heart stops and shows a flat line. The monarchy "died" with the end of the Qing dynasty.

Qín
秦

Qīng
清

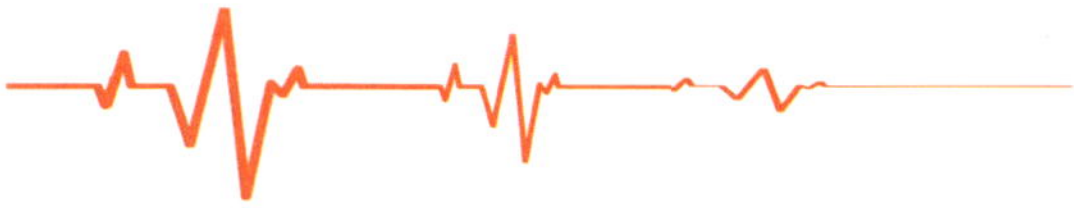

Qin = Chin
Qing = Ching

What is the difference between China and china? Can you give other names referring to China and china in English?

China vs. china

20.4 New words

1. 朝代	cháodài	dynasty
2. 唐尧	Tángyáo	Tangyao (name of a king)
3. 虞舜	Yúshùn	Yushun (name of a king)
4. 夏	Xià	Xia Dynasty
5. 商	Shāng	Shang Dynasty
6. 周	Zhōu	Zhou Dynasty
7. 春秋	Chūnqiū	Spring-Autumn Period
8. 战国	Zhànguó	Warring States Period
9. 乱悠悠	luànyōuyōu	chaos
10. 秦	Qín	Qin Dynasty
11. 汉	Hàn	Han Dynasty
12. 三国	Sānguó	Three Kingdoms
13. 晋	Jìn	Jin Dynasty
14. 统有	tǒngyǒu	united
15. 南朝	Náncháo	Southern Dynasty
16. 北朝	Běicháo	Northern Dynasty
17. 对头	duìtou	in opposition to
18. 隋	Suí	Sui Dynasty
19. 唐	Táng	Tang Dynasty
20. 五代	Wǔdài	Five Dynasties
21. 十国	Shíguó	Ten Kingdoms
22. 宋	Sòng	Song Dynasty
23. 元	Yuán	Yuan Dynasty
24. 明	Míng	Ming Dynasty
25. 清	Qīng	Qing Dynasty
26. 帝王	dìwáng	emperor, king, monarchy
27. 休	xiū	stop, cease

Did you know...

The modern Western name for "China" came from the Italianization of the word "Chin" to which an "a" was added at the end as in the Italian word for the city of Rome: "Roma". When Chinese porcelain (瓷器) became famous, the same word "china" came to be used to refer to porcelain products.

táo
陶
pottery

cí
瓷
porcelain

Vocabulary

阿里山	Ālǐ Shān	a famous mountain in central Taiwan, China	13
哎呀	āiyā	Oh no!	14
埃及	Āijí	Egypt	3
爱	ài	love, like	4
爱护	àihù	treat with care and kindness	12
澳	Ào	abbreviation for Macau	19
澳门	Àomén	Macau	3
八月	bāyuè	August (lit. the 8th month)	11
把	bǎ	*used before the object of a verb*	2
杯	bēi	*a measure word*	16
杯子	bēizi	cup	3
北朝	Běicháo	Northern Dynasty	20
本子	běnzi	notebook	14
比	bǐ	compare	6
比赛	bǐsài	race, competition	10
鞭炮	biānpào	firecracker	9
标	biāo	mark, sign	1
冰	bīng	ice	16
不见	bújiàn	disappear, be gone	14
不算	bú suàn	not considered	18
不能	bù néng	cannot, be unable to	14
部件	bùjiàn	part, component	7
部首	bùshǒu	Chinese character radical	7
草	cǎo	grass, plant	8
长江	Cháng Jiāng	Yangtze River	19
嫦娥	Cháng'é	Chang'e, goddess of the moon	11
钞票	chāopiào	bank note, paper money	14
朝代	cháodài	dynasty	20
车票	chēpiào	ticket for land travel	14
虫	chóng	insect, bug	8
川	chuān	abbreviation for Sichuan Province (lit. river)	19
床	chuáng	bed	8
春秋	Chūnqiū	Spring-Autumn Period	20
从…到…	cóng…dào…	from… to…	15
打球	dǎ qiú	play a ball game	15

Vocabulary

大地	dàdì	earth, land	11
大陆	dàlù	China's mainland	13
带	dài	bring	14
戴	dài	put on	9
单个	dāngè	single	1
岛	dǎo	island	19
到处	dàochù	everywhere	9
地	dì	ground	17
帝王	dìwáng	emperor, king, monarchy	20
点	diǎn	dot	1
碟	dié	plate	19
东北	Dōngběi	Northeast (area of China)	19
咚	dōng	*sound of beating a drum*	9
动物	dòngwù	animal	12
动物园	dòngwùyuán	zoo (lit. animal park)	12
肚子	dùzi	belly, stomach	18
端午节	Duānwǔ Jié	Dragon Boat Festival	10
对头	duìtou	in opposition to	20
多么	duōme	how + adj.	14
鹅	é	goose	2
饿	è	hungry	2
伐	fá	to cut	11
繁体字	fántǐzì	traditional characters	7
放	fàng	set off (fireworks)	9
放过	fàngguò	let go	1
非	fēi	not	1
分	fēn	tell one from another, divide	15
福	fú	abbreviation for Fujian Province (lit. luck, blessing)	19
甘	Gān	abbreviation for Gansu Province (lit. sweet, pleasant, willingly)	19
缸	gāng	vat	6
港	Gǎng	abbreviation for Hong Kong	19
各	gè	each	19
公鸡	gōngjī	rooster, cock	2
狗	gǒu	dog	12
官方	guānfāng	official	1

Vocabulary

广	Guǎng	*Guang* (the first character of the name of the two provinces, 广东 and 广西)	19
贵	Guì	expensive, costly	16
贵	Guì	abbreviation for Guizhou Province (lit. honour, noble, precious)	19
桂	guì	cassia-bark tree, osmanthus, laurel	11
哈哈	hāhā	*sound of laughing*	9
还有	hái yǒu	and, additionally	14
海	hǎi	sea	3
海鸥	hǎi'ōu	seagull	3
海洋	hǎiyáng	ocean	11
汉	Hàn	Han Dynasty	20
好笑	hǎoxiào	funny	18
红包	hóngbāo	red packet, lucky money as a gift	9
猴子	hóuzi	monkey	18
湖	Hú	*Hu* (the first character of the name of the two provinces, 湖北 and 湖南)	19
沪	Hù	abbreviation for Shanghai	19
花	huā	flower	5
画画儿	huà huàr	draw	4
黄河	Huáng Hé	Yellow River	19
回家	huí jiā	return home, go home	14
虫	huǐ	the radical indicating insects and bugs	8
火	huǒ	fire	8
纪念	jìniàn	commemorate or memorialize	10
加	jiā	plus, add	19
假牙	jiǎyá	false teeth	4
简体字	jiǎntǐzì	simplified characters	7
简易	jiǎnyì	simple and easy	1
教	jiāo	teach	15
叫	jiào	sound made by a rooster, to crow	2
金	jīn	gold, metal	8
津	Jīn	abbreviation for Tianjin	19
晋	Jìn	Jin Dynasty	20
京	Jīng	abbreviation for Beijing	19
看戏	kàn xì	watch a show or play	17
慷慨	kāngkǎi	generous	18
快	kuài	soon, before long	2

Vocabulary

老奶奶	lǎonǎinai	old lady, grandma	18
龙船	lóngchuán	dragon boat	10
乱悠悠	luànyōuyōu	chaos	20
买	mǎi	buy	16
帽	mào	hat	9
民族	mínzú	ethnic group	19
明	Míng	Ming Dynasty	20
明年	míngnián	next year	13
明天	míngtiān	tomorrow	17
木	mù	wood, tree	8
南朝	Náncháo	Southern Dynasty	20
年糕	niángāo	New Year's cake	9
牛油	niúyóu	butter	3
欧洲	Ōuzhōu	Europe	3
陪	péi	accompany	15
盆	pén	basin	6
皮	pí	skin, peel	17
便宜	piányi	cheap, inexpensive	16
平安	píng'ān	peace, peaceful	19
浅	qiǎn	shallow	6
锵	qiāng	*sound of a gong clanking*	9
秦	Qín	Qin Dynasty	20
清	Qīng	Qing Dynasty	20
请	qǐng	ask somebody to do something, invite	17
庆祝	qìngzhù	celebrate	11
屈原	Qū Yuán	Qu Yuan (name of a great poet)	10
热闹	rènao	bustling with noise and excitement, lively	9
三国	Sānguó	Three Kingdoms	20
三轮车	sānlúnchē	rickshaw	18
陕	Shǎn	abbreviation for Shaanxi Province (lit. narrow path)	19
商	Shāng	Shang Dynasty	20
赏	shǎng	enjoy, appreciate	11
上学	shàng xué	go to school	14
深	shēn	deep	6
神	shén	god or deity	13

Vocabulary

神木	shén mù	sacred tree	13
生气	shēng qì	get angry	17
声调	shēngdiào	tone	1
省	shěng	province	19
十国	Shíguó	Ten Kingdoms	20
手机	shǒujī	mobile phone (lit. hand phone)	14
书法	shūfǎ	calligraphy	7
丝	sī	silk, fabric	8
宋	Sòng	Song Dynasty	20
送	sòng	hand something to somebody (as a gift)	5
隋	Suí	Sui Dynasty	20
唐	Táng	Tang Dynasty	20
唐尧	Tángyáo	Tangyao (name of a king)	20
统有	tǒngyǒu	united	20
土	tǔ	earth, ground	8
娃娃	wáwa	baby, child	4
玩具	wánjù	toy	12
碗	wǎn	bowl	6
文具袋	wénjùdài	pencil case	14
乌龟	wūguī	turtle	3
无	wú	not have, without	1
吴刚	Wú Gāng	Wu Gang (name of a person)	11
五代	Wǔdài	Five Dynasties	20
五月	wǔyuè	May (lit. the 5th month)	10
午饭	wǔfàn	lunch	14
喜欢	xǐhuan	to like	5
夏	Xià	Xia Dynasty	20
相伴	xiāng bàn	companion, keep somebody company	11
香袋	xiāng dài	fragrant bag, sachet	10
象形字	xiàngxíngzì	pictogram, pictorial characters	7
小姐	xiǎojiě	young lady, Miss	17
笑	xiào	laugh	9
形声字	xíngshēngzì	pictophonetic characters	7
熊猫	xióngmāo	panda	12
休	xiū	stop, cease	20

Vocabulary

呀	ya	Ah! or Oh!	5
烟花	yānhuā	fireworks	9
艺术	yìshù	art (as an abstract concept)	7
渝	Yú	abbreviation for Chongqing	20
虞舜	Yúshùn	Yushun (name of a king)	20
与	yǔ	and, with	1
语言	yǔyán	language	1
玉兔	yùtù	Jade Rabbit	11
元	Yuán	Yuan Dynasty	19
元音	yuányīn	vowel	1
月饼	yuèbing	mooncake	11
月宫	yuègōng	Moon Palace	11
月亮	yuèliang	moon	11
云	yún	abbreviation for Yunnan Province (lit. cloud)	19
运动服	yùndòngfú	sportswear	14
怎么好	zěnme hǎo	What shall I do to solve this problem?	14
战国	Zhànguó	Warring States Period	20
张	Zhāng	open	2
找	zhǎo	look for, search	1
找到	zhǎodào	find (something missing)	14
找钱	zhǎo qián	give change	16
照	zhào	shine	11
吱吱	zhīzhī	eeh, eeh (*sound a monkey makes*)	18
中秋节	Zhōngqiū Jié	Mid-Autumn Festival	11
种	zhòng	to plant	5
周	Zhōu	Zhou Dynasty	20
竹	zhú	bamboo	8
自治区	zìzhìqū	autonomous region	19
字母	zìmǔ	alphabetical letters	1
粽子	zòngzi	sticky rice dumpling usually wrapped in bamboo leaves	10
足	zú	foot, feet	8
最	zuì	most, superlatively	6

图书在版编目（CIP）数据

嘻哈说唱学汉语 · 4/卢毓文著.
—北京：北京语言大学出版社，2010.12
ISBN 978-7-5619-2627-7

Ⅰ. 嘻… Ⅱ. 卢… Ⅲ. 汉语—对外汉语教学—教材 Ⅳ. H195.4

中国版本图书馆CIP数据核字（2010）第254460号

书　　名：嘻哈说唱学汉语 · 4
责任印制：汪学发

出版发行：北京语言大学出版社
社　　址：北京市海淀区学院路15号　　邮政编码：100083
网　　址：www.blcup.com
电　　话：发行部 82303648/3591/3651
　　　　　编辑部 82303647
　　　　　读者服务部 82303653/3908
　　　　　网上订购电话 82303668
　　　　　客户服务信箱 service@blcup.net
印　　刷：北京联兴盛业印刷股份有限公司
经　　销：全国新华书店

版　　次：2011年2月第1版　　2011年2月第1次印刷
开　　本：889毫米 × 1194毫米　1/16　　印张：6.25
字　　数：85千字
书　　号：ISBN 978-7-5619-2627-7/H·10335
　　　　　06800

凡有印装质量问题，本社出版部负责调换。电话：82303590
Printed in China